HISTORICAL ATLAS
OF THE WORLD

Barnes & Noble, Inc., New York
Publishers · Booksellers · Since 1873

This edition © Barnes & Noble Inc., New York
and
W. & R. Chambers Ltd., Edinburgh 1970

Reprinted 1971

Original edition © J. W. Cappelens Forlag A/S
Oslo 1962

The original Norwegian edition was prepared by
Oddvar Bjørklund, Haakon Holmboe and Anders Røhr
with maps by Berit Lie.

SBN: 389 00253 4 (paper)
389 01087 1 (cloth)

The publishers wish to record their gratitude to Haakon and Lotte
Holmboe, who cooperated in the preparation of this edition, and
to many teachers and lecturers in history who gave advice.

Library of Congress Catalog Card Number 78-80004

Printed in Holland by The Ysel Press, Deventer

FOREWORD

This *Historical Atlas of the World* has been designed for students in schools and universities—and anyone interested in history. It is informative and reliable yet attractively clear and handy to use.

The obvious aim is to illustrate history with the help of maps. The particular aim is not simply to localize past events geographically but to show the dynamic, the movement and the progress of history—the growth and decline of empires; the migration of races and nations; the encroachment of conquerors and the course of wars; the shifting of national boundaries; the fluctuating power structures between nations or religions; the growth of cultural and political movements— and much more. On several pages a number of individual maps, linked by a main theme, illustrate specific cultural and political developments.

Here, then, is history projected in maps instead of the written word—and maps such as these can fire the imagination as well.

CONTENTS ANCIENT TIMES
From the dawn of civilization to the
time of the Roman emperors
Maps 1 to 31

CONTENTS THE MIDDLE AGES
From the Barbarian migrations to
the great voyages of discovery
Maps 32 to 55

CONTENTS   RECENT TIMES
From Charles V to Bismarck
Maps 56 to 93

CONTENTS   THE TWENTIETH CENTURY
From the Boer War to the present day
Maps 94 to 108

ABBREVIATIONS

AB.	Archbishopric
A.D.	Archduchy
B.	Bishopric
C.	County
c.	*circa*
D.	Duchy
Dsp.	Despotate
EL.	Electorate
exp.	expedition
G.D.	Grand Duchy
I., Is.	Island(s)
K.	Kingdom
LG.	Landgraviate
MG.	Margraviate
mod	modern name
Mt., Mts.	Mount, Mountain(s)
Pr.	Principality
Prov.	Province
Rep.	Republic

Index   follows Map 108

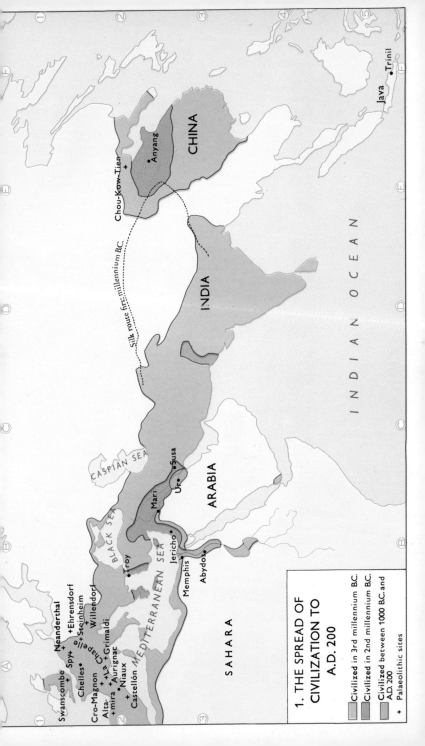

1. THE SPREAD OF CIVILIZATION TO A.D. 200

Civilized in 3rd millennium B.C.
Civilized in 2nd millennium B.C.
Civilized between 1000 B.C. and A.D. 200
+ Palaeolithic sites

CHINA
Chou-Kow-Tien
Anyang

INDIA
Silk route first millennium B.C.

Java
Trinil

INDIAN OCEAN

ARABIA
Susa
Ur
Mari
Jericho
Memphis
Abydos
Troy
BLACK SEA
CASPIAN SEA
MEDITERRANEAN SEA
SAHARA

Swanscombe
Neanderthal
Spy
Ehrensdorf
Chelles
Steinheim
Cro-Magnon
Willendorf
Alta
La Chapelle
Grimaldi
mira
Aurignac
Niaux
Castellón

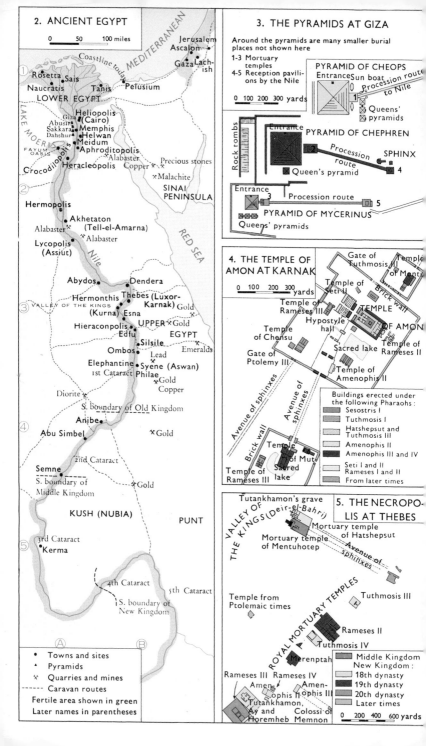

2. ANCIENT EGYPT

0   50   100 miles

MEDITERRANEAN

Coastline today

Rosetta, Sais
Naucratis
LOWER EGYPT
Tanis
Pelusium

Jerusalem
Ascalon
Gaza Lachish

Heliopolis
(Cairo)
Giza
Abusir
Sakkara Memphis
Dahshur Helwan
Meidum
Aphroditopolis
Heracleopolis

Alabaster
Copper ×Precious stones
×Malachite

SINAI
PENINSULA

Hermopolis
Akhetaton
(Tell-el-Amarna)
Alabaster×
×Alabaster
Lycopolis
(Assiût)

RED SEA

Abydos
Dendera
Hermonthis Thebes (Luxor-
(Kurna) Karnak) Gold
VALLEY OF THE KINGS
Esna
Hieraconpolis
UPPER
Edfu
EGYPT
Silsile
Ombos
Emeralds
Lead
Elephantine
Syene (Aswan)
1st Cataract Philae
Gold
Diorite×
Copper

S. boundary of Old Kingdom

Anibe
×Gold

Abu Simbel

2nd Cataract

Semne
×Gold
S. boundary of
Middle Kingdom

KUSH (NUBIA)

PUNT

3rd Cataract
Kerma

4th Cataract
5th Cataract
S. boundary of
New Kingdom

FAYUM OASIS
LAKE MOERIS
Crocodilopolis

• Towns and sites
▲ Pyramids
× Quarries and mines
--- Caravan routes
Fertile area shown in green
Later names in parentheses

3. THE PYRAMIDS AT GIZA

Around the pyramids are many smaller burial
places not shown here

1-3 Mortuary
temples
4-5 Reception pavili-
ons by the Nile

0 100 200 300 yards

PYRAMID OF CHEOPS
Entrance Sun boat Procession route
to Nile
Queens'
pyramids

Rock tombs

PYRAMID OF CHEPHREN
Entrance
Procession
route
SPHINX
Queen's pyramid

Entrance
Procession route
PYRAMID OF MYCERINUS
Queens' pyramids

4. THE TEMPLE OF AMON AT KARNAK

0 100 200 300 yards

Gate of
Tuthmosis III
Temple
of Month

Temple of
Seti II
Brick wall

Temple of
Rameses III
TEMPLE
Hypostyle
hall
OF AMON

Temple
of Chensu
Sacred lake
Temple of
Rameses II

Gate of
Ptolemy III
Temple of
Amenophis II

Avenue of sphinxes
Avenue of sphinxes

Brick wall

Temple
of Mut
Sacred
lake
Temple of
Rameses III

Buildings erected under
the following Pharaohs:

Sesostris I
Tuthmosis I
Hatshepsut and
Tuthmosis III
Amenophis II
Amenophis III and IV
Seti I and II
Rameses I and II
From later times

5. THE NECROPOLIS AT THEBES

Tutankhamon's grave
VALLEY OF THE KINGS (Deir-el-Bahri)
Mortuary temple
of Hatshepsut
Mortuary temple
of Mentuhotep
Avenue of
sphinxes

Temple from
Ptolemaic times
Tuthmosis III

ROYAL MORTUARY TEMPLES
Rameses II
Tuthmosis IV
Merenptah

Rameses III Rameses IV
Amen-
ophis II
Amen-
ophis III
Tutankhamon,
Ay and
Horemheb
Colossi of
Memnon

Middle Kingdom
New Kingdom:
18th dynasty
19th dynasty
20th dynasty
Later times

0 200 400 600 yards

Map 6: THE NEAR EAST c. 1400 B.C.

BLACK SEA
SEA OF MARMARA
Troy
PHRYGIA
• (Alaça Hüyük)
• Hattushash (Bogaz-Köy)
HITTITE EMPIRE
Kanesh
• Sardes
(Malatya)
(Maras)
(Zincirli) • Sakjegözü
Tarsus AMO
Amanus
(Atchana) • Carchemish
Alalakh
Ugarit
(Ras Shamra)
Haleb
(Aleppo)
Rhodes
MINOAN-MYCENAEAN
TERRITORY
Cyprus
MEDITERRANEAN
SEA
Qatna
Byblos • Kadesh
Sidon • Damascus
Tyre
Megiddo
Ascalon • Jerusalem
Lachish
Memphis
LAKE MOERIS
FAYUM
SINAI
(Tell-el-Amarna)
E G Y P T I A N   E M P I R E
RED SEA
Nile
Thebes
COLCHIS
CAUCASUS
* Ararat
ASSYRIA
MITANNI
Nineveh • Great Zab
Arbela
Ashur • Little Zab
Tigris
KASSITES
MESOPOTAMIA
Mari • Euphrates
SYRIAN DESERT
ARABIA
Sippar • Babylon
Kish
Nippur • Lagash
Urek
Larsa
Ur
BABYLONIA
ELAM

6. THE NEAR EAST
c. 1400 B.C.
Later names are in parentheses
0   100   200   300 miles

7. THE EAST
c. 600 B.C.
■ Lydian Kingdom
■ Median Kingdom
■ Neo-Babylonian Empire
— Greatest extent of Assyrian
Empire c. 700 B.C.
0   200   400 miles

BLACK SEA
CASPIAN SEA
LYDIA
Sardes
Miletus
PISIDIA
CILICIA
ARMENIA
Cyrus
Rhodes
Cyprus
MEDITERRANEAN SEA
SYRIA
Sidon
Tyre • Damascus
MESOPOTAMIA
ASSYRIA
Tigris
Euphrates
MEDIA
Ecbatana
PARTHIA
BACTRIA
ARIA
ARACHOSIA
BABY-LONIA
Babylon • Susa
Sais • Gaza
GOSHEN
Memphis
EGYPT
Thebes
RED SEA
Nile
ARABIA
PERSIA
PERSIAN GULF
GEDROSIA
Indus

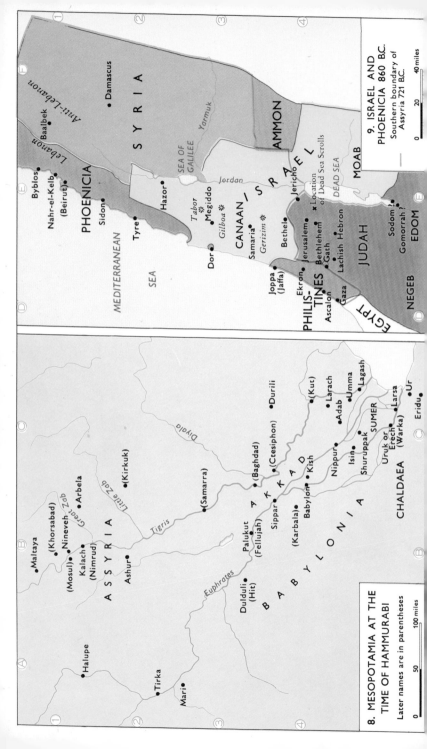

8. MESOPOTAMIA AT THE TIME OF HAMMURABI

Later names are in parentheses

0   50   100 miles

Halupe

Tirka

Mari

ASSYRIA

Maltaya

(Mosul) • Nineveh (Nimrud)
(Khorsabad) • Arbela
Kalach (Nimrud)
Ashur

(Kirkuk)

Great Zab

Little Zab

Tigris

(Samarra)

Diyala

(Baghdad)

• Durili

A K K A D

Palukut (Fellujah)

Sippar

(Ctesiphon)

(Kut)

Euphrates

Dulduli (Hit)

BABYLONIA

(Karbala) Babylon

Kish

Larach

Umma

Lagash

Adab

Nippur

SUMER

Isin

Shuruppak

Uruk or
Erech
(Warka)

Larsa

CHALDAEA

Eridu

Ur

9. ISRAEL AND PHOENICIA 860 B.C.

Southern boundary of
Assyria 721 B.C.

——

0   20   40 miles

Anti-Lebanon

• Damascus

Baalbek

Lebanon

S Y R I A

PHOENICIA

Byblos

Nahr-el-Kelb
(Beirut)

Sidon

Tyre

MEDITERRANEAN
SEA

Hazor

SEA OF
GALILEE

Yarmuk

AMMON

Dor

Jordan

Tabor ✸
Megiddo ✸
Gilboa

CANAAN

Samaria

Gerizim ✸

I S R A E L

Bethel

Jericho

× Location
of Dead Sea Scrolls

Jerusalem

Bethlehem

DEAD SEA

Joppa
(Jaffa)

Ekron

Gath

PHILIS-
TINES

Ascalon

Gaza

Lachish Hebron

JUDAH

MOAB

Sodom ?

Gomorrah ?

EDOM

NEGEB

EGYPT

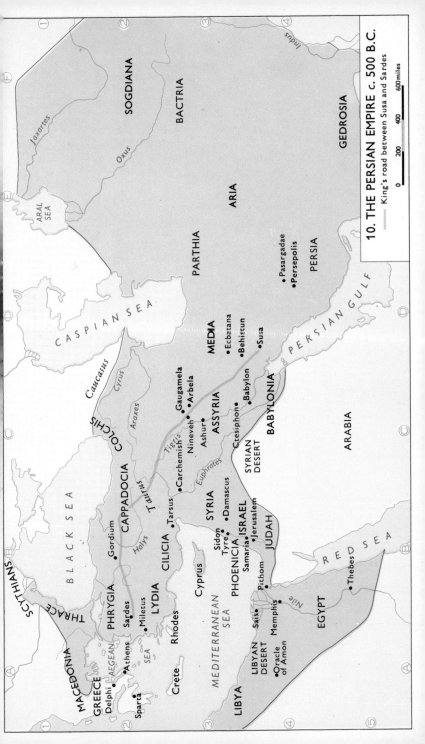

10. THE PERSIAN EMPIRE c. 500 B.C.

—— King's road between Susa and Sardes

0   200   400   600 miles

Labels

SCYTHIANS

THRACE
MACEDONIA
GREECE
Delphi
Athens
Sparta

AEGEAN SEA

BLACK SEA

PHRYGIA
Gordium
LYDIA
Sardes
Miletus
Rhodes
Crete
Cyprus

CILICIA
Tarsus
Halys
Taurus

CAPPADOCIA

COLCHIS
Caucasus
Cyrus
Araxes

CASPIAN SEA

ARAL SEA

Jaxartes

SOGDIANA

Oxus

BACTRIA

PARTHIA

ARIA

GEDROSIA

MEDIA
Ecbatana
Behistun
Susa

PERSIA
Pasargadae
Persepolis

PERSIAN GULF

Tigris
Carchemish
Nineveh
Ashur
ASSYRIA
Gaugamela
Arbela

Euphrates
Ctesiphon
Babylon
BABYLONIA

SYRIA
Damascus
SYRIAN DESERT

ARABIA

MEDITERRANEAN SEA

Sidon
Tyre
PHOENICIA
Samaria
ISRAEL
Jerusalem
JUDAH

Pithom

EGYPT
Saïs
Memphis
Libyan Desert
Oracle of Amon
LIBYA
Nile
Thebes

RED SEA

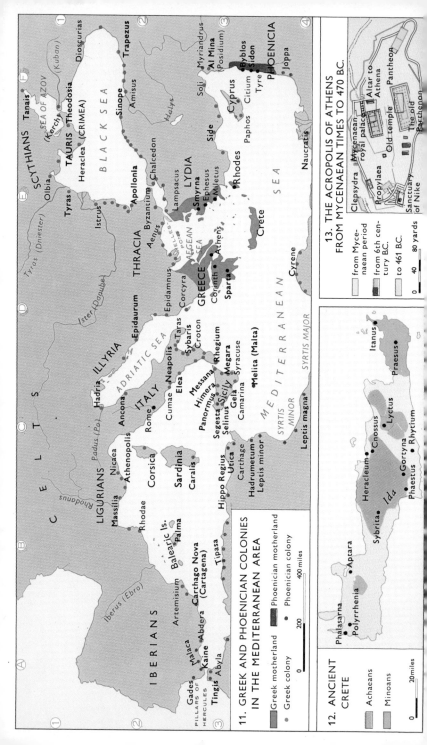

11. GREEK AND PHOENICIAN COLONIES IN THE MEDITERRANEAN AREA

Greek motherland
Phoenician motherland
• Greek colony
• Phoenician colony

0   200   400 miles

12. ANCIENT CRETE

Achaeans
Minoans

0   20 miles

13. THE ACROPOLIS OF ATHENS FROM MYCENAEAN TIMES TO 470 B.C.

from Mycenaean period
from 6th century B.C.
to 461 B.C.

0   40   80 yards

14. ANCIENT GREECE

Greek peoples:

- Ionians
- Dorians
- Aeolians
- Northwest Greeks (North Dorians)
- Arcadians

0   20   40   60 miles

15. CENTRAL GREECE

0   10   20 miles

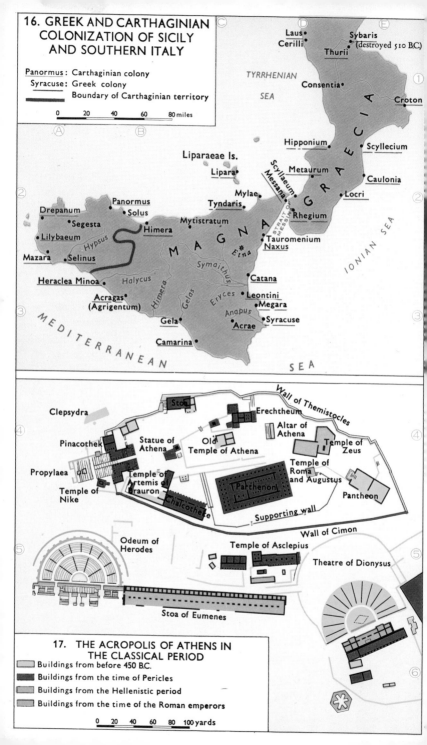

16. GREEK AND CARTHAGINIAN COLONIZATION OF SICILY AND SOUTHERN ITALY

Panrmus: Carthaginian colony
Syracuse: Greek colony
Boundary of Carthaginian territory

0   20   40   60   80 miles

TYRRHENIAN SEA

Laus
Cerilli
Sybaris (destroyed 510 B.C.)
Thurii
Consentia
Croton

Liparaeae Is.
Lipara

Hipponium
Scyllecium
Metaurum
Caulonia
Scyllaeum
Mylae
Messana
Locri
Tyndaris
Rhegium

Drepanum
Panormus
Solus
Segesta
Mytistratum
Lilybaeum
Himera
Mazara
Selinus
Hypsus
Tauromenium
Naxus
Etna
Heraclea Minoa
Halycus
Symaithus
Acragas (Agrigentum)
Himera
Gelas
Eryces
Catana
Leontini
Megara
Anapus
Gela
Acrae
Syracuse
Camarina

MAGNA GRAECIA

STRAIT OF MESSINA

IONIAN SEA

MEDITERRANEAN SEA

Wall of Themistocles

Clepsydra
Stoa
Erechtheum
Altar of Athena
Pinacothek
Statue of Athena
Old Temple of Athena
Temple of Zeus
Propylaea
Temple of Artemis of Brauron
Temple of Roma and Augustus
Temple of Nike
Chalcotheke
Parthenon
Pantheon
Supporting wall
Wall of Cimon

Odeum of Herodes
Temple of Asclepius
Theatre of Dionysus
Stoa of Eumenes

17. THE ACROPOLIS OF ATHENS IN THE CLASSICAL PERIOD

Buildings from before 450 B.C.
Buildings from the time of Pericles
Buildings from the Hellenistic period
Buildings from the time of the Roman emperors

0   20   40   60   80 100 yards

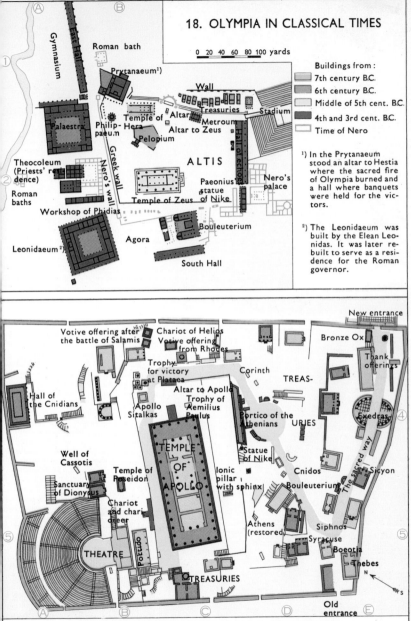

18. OLYMPIA IN CLASSICAL TIMES

0 20 40 60 80 100 yards

Gymnasium

Roman bath

East Hall

Prytanaeum[1]

Roman baths

Theocoleum (Priests' residence)

Palaestra

Philip-paeum

Temple of Hera

Pelopium

Wall

Treasuries

Altar

Metroum

Altar to Zeus

Stadium

Hall of Echoes

ALTIS

Workshop of Phidias

Temple of Zeus

Paeonius' statue of Nike

Nero's palace

Greek wall

Nero's wall

Leonidaeum[2]

Agora

Bouleuterium

South Hall

Buildings from:
- 7th century B.C.
- 6th century B.C.
- Middle of 5th cent. B.C.
- 4th and 3rd cent. B.C.
- Time of Nero

[1]) In the Prytanaeum stood an altar to Hestia where the sacred fire of Olympia burned and a hall where banquets were held for the victors.

[2]) The Leonidaeum was built by the Elean Leonidas. It was later rebuilt to serve as a residence for the Roman governor.

Votive offering after the battle of Salamis

Chariot of Helios

Votive offering from Rhodes

Bronze Ox

Thank offerings

Trophy for victory at Plataea

Corinth

TREAS-

Hall of the Cnidians

Apollo Sitalkas

Altar to Apollo

Trophy of Aemilius Paulus

Portico of the Athenians

URIES

Exedras

Well of Cassotis

Temple of Poseidon

TEMPLE OF APOLLO

Statue of Nike

Ionic pillar with sphinx

Cnidos

Sicyon

The sacred way

Sanctuary of Dionysus

Chariot and charioteer

Bouleuterium

Siphnos

Athens (restored)

Syracuse

THEATRE

Portico

Boeotia

Thebes

TREASURIES

New entrance

Old entrance

N S

19. THE SANCTUARY OF APOLLO AT DELPHI

- Buildings and monuments from before 525 B.C.
- Buildings and monuments from 525-448 B.C.
- Buildings and monuments from 423-321 B.C.
- Buildings and monuments from the period after 321 B.C.

THE TEMPLE OF APOLLO

Destroyed by fire in 548 B.C. Rebuilt magnificently from c. 515 B.C. by the Alcmaeonids. Destroyed by an earthquake in 373 B.C. Rebuilt once more 370-330 B.C.

0 10 20 30 40 50 yards

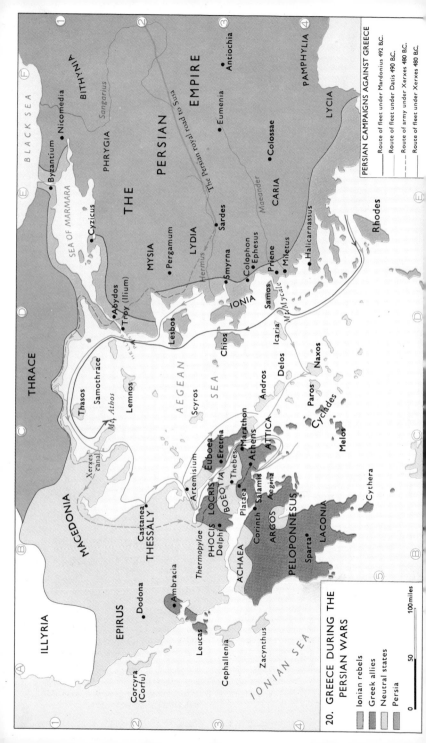

20. GREECE DURING THE PERSIAN WARS

PERSIAN CAMPAIGNS AGAINST GREECE

—— Route of fleet under Mardonius 492 B.C.
—— Route of fleet under Datis 490 B.C.
- - - Route of army under Xerxes 480 B.C.
—— Route of fleet under Xerxes 480 B.C.

Ionian rebels
Greek allies
Neutral states
Persia

0   50   100 miles

ILLYRIA

THRACE

EPIRUS
Corcyra (Corfu)
Dodona
Ambracia
Leucas
Cephallenia
Zacynthus

MACEDONIA
Castanea
Xerxes canal
Mt Athos
Thasos
Samothrace
Lemnos
Scyros

THESSALY
Thermopylae
PHOCIS
Delphi
LOCRIS
BOEOTIA
ACHAEA
Plataea
Thebes
Corinth
ARGOS
Sparta
LACONIA
PELOPONNESUS
Cythera

Artemisium
Euboea
Eretria
Marathon
ATTICA
Athens
Salamis
Aegina

AEGEAN SEA
Andros
Delos
Paros
Cyclades
Melos
Naxos
Icaria

Lesbos
Chios
Samos
Mt Mycale
Rhodes

THE PERSIAN EMPIRE

BLACK SEA

SEA OF MARMARA
Byzantium
Nicomedia
BITHYNIA
Cyzicus
PHRYGIA
Sangarius

Abydos
Troy (Ilium)
HELLESPONT

MYSIA
Pergamum
LYDIA
Sardes
Smyrna
Hermus
IONIA
Colophon
Ephesus
Priene
Miletus
Halicarnassus
CARIA
Meander

The Persian royal road to Susa
Antiochia
Eumenia
Colossae
PAMPHYLIA
LYCIA

IONIAN SEA

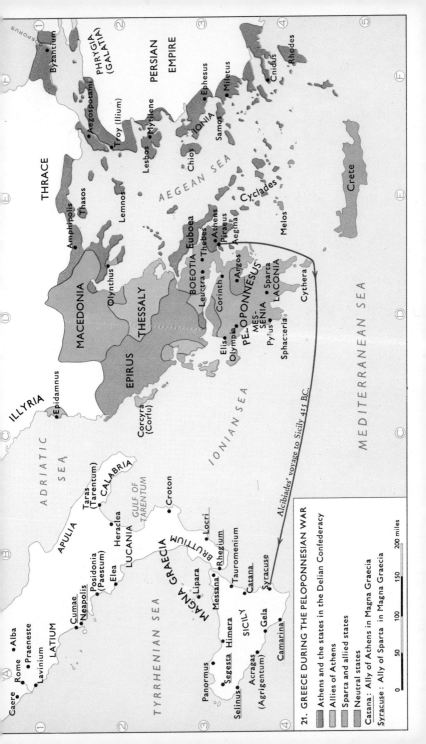

21. GREECE DURING THE PELOPONNESIAN WAR

Athens and the states in the Delian Confederacy
Allies of Athens
Sparta and allied states
Neutral states

Catana: Ally of Athens in Magna Graecia
Syracuse: Ally of Sparta in Magna Graecia

0   50   100   150   200 miles

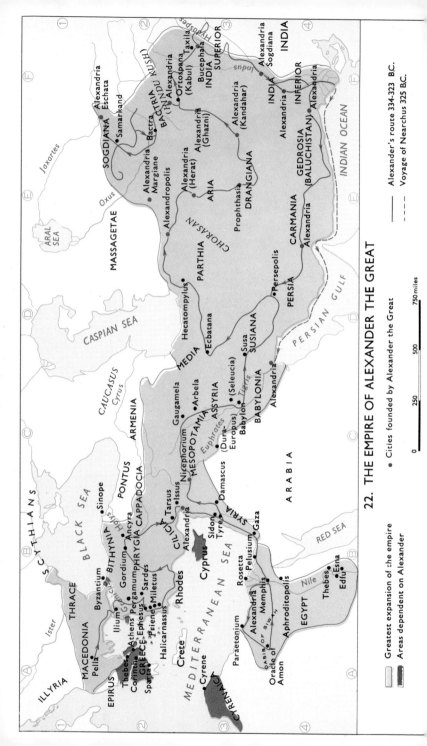

22. THE EMPIRE OF ALEXANDER THE GREAT

Greatest expansion of the empire

Areas dependent on Alexander

● Cities founded by Alexander the Great

——— Alexander's route 334–323 B.C.

- - - - Voyage of Nearchus 325 B.C.

0   250   500   750 miles

23. ITALY BEFORE THE FIRST PUNIC WAR 264 B.C.

- Etruscans
- Greek colonies
- Carthaginian dominions
- Italians
- Other peoples
- Gallic territory
- Southern and northern boundaries of Roman territory 264 B.C.
- Important Roman roads and roads built after 264 B.C.

0   50   100   150 miles

GALLIA TRANSPADANA
Mediolanum
Verona
Vercellae
VENETIA
Patavium
Augusta Taurinorum
Mantua
Cremona
Placentia
Pola
Padus
LIGURIA
Parma
Mutina
GALLIA
Bononia
Via Aemilia
Genua
CISPADANA
Ravenna
Nicaea
Rubico
Ariminum
Pisa
Arnus
Florentia
Sena
Ancona
Ilva
Arretium
ETRURIA
Perusia
UMBRIA
Camerinum
PICENUM
Asculum
CORSICA
Aleria
Vulci
Tarquinii
Veii
SABINI
AEQUI
Via Valeria
Corfinium
Caere
Fidenae
Ostia
Rome
Praeneste
LATIUM
VOLSCI
SAMNIUM
APULIA
Cannae
Terracina
Capua
Beneventum
Neapolis
Via Appia
SARDINIA
Pithecussa
Pompeii
Vesuvius
Brundisium
Puteoli
Paestum
Tarentum
Herculaneum
CAMPANIA
LUCANIA
CALABRIA
Neapolis
Heraclea
Carales
Sybaris
TYRRHENIAN SEA
BRUTTIUM
Croton
Liparaeae Is.
IONIAN SEA
Aegates Is.
Panormus
Messana
Lilybaeum
Segesta
Rhegium
SICILY
Etna
Catana (Catania)
AFRICA
Agrigentum (Acragas)
Gela
Syracuse
Utica
Carthage

24. THE RETREAT OF THE TEN THOUSAND 401-399 B.C.

Route followed by the Greeks, first under the leadership of Cyrus, later under Xenophon

0   100   200 miles

Byzantium (399 B.C.)
Sinope
Heraclea
Abydos
Cotyora
Cerasus
Trapezus
CAUCASUS
Pergamum
CAPPADOCIA
PONTUS
Araxes
LYDIA
Sardes
PHRYGIA
ARMENIA (400 B.C.)
Ephesus
Priene
Miletus
Iconium
PERSIAN
Tyana
EMPIRE
MEDIA
Rhodes
CILICIA
(KURDISTAN)
Tarsus
Myriandrus
ASSYRIA
Mespila (Nineveh)
Thapsacus
MEDITERRANEAN SEA
MESOPOTAMIA
Cyprus
Euphrates
Tigris
Sidon
Damascus
Cunaxa (401 B.C.)
Sittace
Babylon
Jerusalem
ARABIA
BABYLONIA
Halys

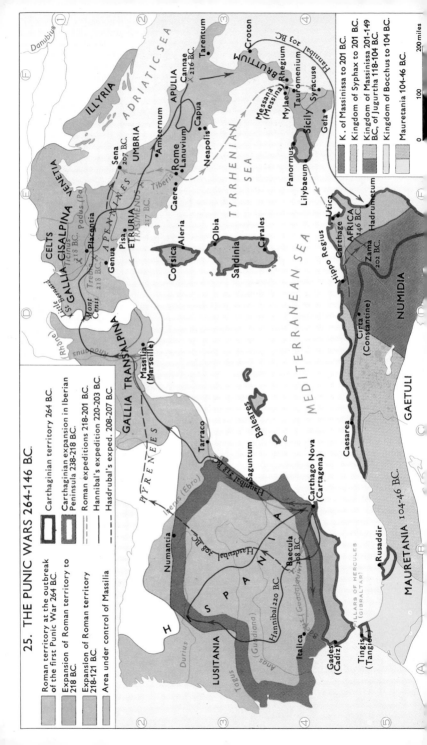

25. THE PUNIC WARS 264-146 B.C.

Roman territory at the outbreak of the first Punic War 264 B.C.

Expansion of Roman territory to 218 B.C.

Expansion of Roman territory 218-121 B.C.

Area under control of Massilia

Carthaginian territory 264 B.C.

Carthaginian expansion in Iberian Peninsula 238-218 B.C.

Roman expeditions 218-201 B.C.

Hannibal's expedition 220-203 B.C.

Hasdrubal's exped. 208-207 B.C.

K. of Massinissa to 201 B.C.

Kingdom of Syphax to 201 B.C.

Kingdom of Massinissa 201-149 B.C., of Jugurtha 118-104 B.C.

Kingdom of Bocchus to 104 B.C.

Mauretania 104-46 B.C.

0   100   200 miles

F — Danubius

ADRIATIC SEA

ILLYRIA

VENETIA

GALLIA CISALPINA

CELTS

Little Bernard

St Bernard

Mont Cenis

Trebia 218 B.C.

Placentia 218 B.C.

Ticinus 218 B.C.

Genua

Pisa

APENNINES

Padus (Po)

Sena 207 B.C.

UMBRIA

Amiternum

Tiberis

ETRURIA

Trasimenus 217 B.C.

Caere

Rome

Lanuvium

Capua

Neapolis

Cannae X 216 B.C.

APULIA

Tarentum

Croton

BRUTTIUM

Hannibal 203 for B.C.

Rhegium

Tauromenium

Messana (Messina)

Mylae

Syracuse

Sicily

Gela

Panormus

Lilybaeum

TYRRHENIAN SEA

Corsica

Aleria

Olbia

Carales

Sardinia

GALLIA TRANSALPINA

Rhône

Durance

Massilia (Marseille)

PYRENEES

Tarraco

Saguntum

Baleares

Carthago Nova (Cartagena)

MEDITERRANEAN SEA

H

LUSITANIA

Durius

Tagus

Anas (Guadiana)

Numantia

Hannibal 220 B.C.

Italica

Gades (Cadiz)

PILLARS OF HERCULES (GIBRALTAR)

Tingis (Tangier)

Rusadir

Baecula 208 B.C.

Hasdrubal 208 B.C.

Iberus (Ebro)

Hannibal 218 B.C.

S P A N I A

Caesarea

MAURETANIA 104-46 B.C.

GAETULI

Hippo Regius

Utica

Carthage

AFRICA 146 B.C.

Hadrumetum

Zama 202 B.C.

Cirta (Constantine)

NUMIDIA

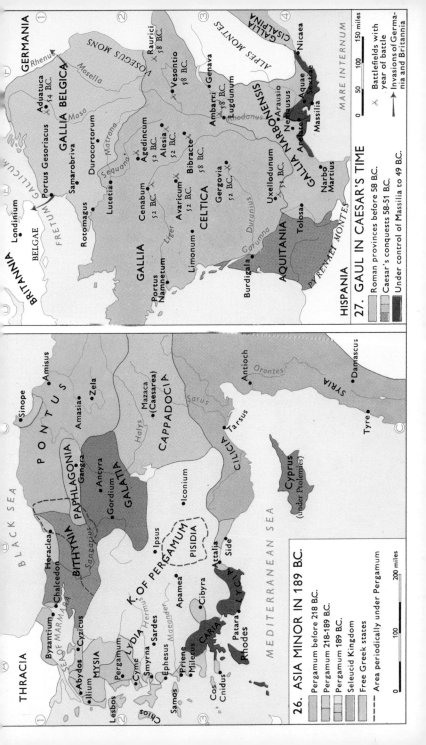

26. ASIA MINOR IN 189 B.C.

THRACIA

BLACK SEA

Sinope

Amisus

P O N T U S

Heraclea
Chalcedon
Byzantium

PAPHLAGONIA

Gangra

Amasia

Zela

Amasia

Abydos
Ilium
Cyzicus

BITHYNIA

Sangarius

Ancyra

GALATIA

Gordium

Ipsus

Mazaca
(Caesarea)

CAPPADOCIA

Halys

Sarus

Antioch

Orontes

SYRIA

Damascus

SEA OF MARMARA

Pergamum

MYSIA

K. OF PERGAMUM

Lesbos

Cyme

Smyrna

Sardes

LYDIA

Hermus

Iconium

PISIDIA

CILICIA

Tarsus

Cyprus
(under Ptolemy)

Tyre

Ephesus
Priene
Miletus

Samos

CARIA

Apamea

Maeander

Cibyra

Attalia

Side

Patara

LYCIA

Chios

Cos
Cnidus

Rhodes

MEDITERRANEAN SEA

Pergamum before 218 B.C.
Pergamum 218–189 B.C.
Pergamum 189 B.C.
Seleucid Kingdom
Free Greek states
Area periodically under Pergamum

0   100   200 miles

27. GAUL IN CAESAR'S TIME

GERMANIA

Rhenus

BRITANNIA

Londinium

BELGAE

GALLIA

GALLICUM

FRETUM

Portus Gesoriacus

GALLIA BELGICA

Aduatuca ✕ 54 B.C.

Mosella

Mosa

Rauricis ✕ 58 B.C.

VOSEGUS MONS

Vesontio ✕ 58 B.C.

Samarobriva

Durocortorum

Agedincum ✕ 52 B.C.

Matrona

Rotomagus

Luetia

Sequana

Cenabum ✕ 52 B.C.

Alesia ✕ 52 B.C.

Bibracte ✕ 58 B.C.

CELTICA

GALLIA

Avaricum ✕ 52 B.C.

Gergovia ✕ 52 B.C.

Uxellodunum ✕ 51 B.C.

Ambarri

Genava

Lugdunum

Rhodanus

Arausio ✕ 18 B.C.

Nemausus

ALPES MONTES

GALLIA CISALPINA

Nicaea

Aquae Sextiae ✕

Massilia

Antipolis

Arelate

GALLIA NARBONENSIS

Narbo Martius

Tolosa

AQUITANIA

Burdigala

Garunna

Duranius

PYRENAEI MONTES

Limonum

Portus Namnetum

Liger

GALLIA

HISPANIA

MARE INTERNUM

✕ Battlefields with year of battle

→ Invasions of Germania and Britannia

Roman provinces before 58 B.C.
Caesar's conquests 58–51 B.C.
Under control of Massilia to 49 B.C.

0   50   100   150 miles

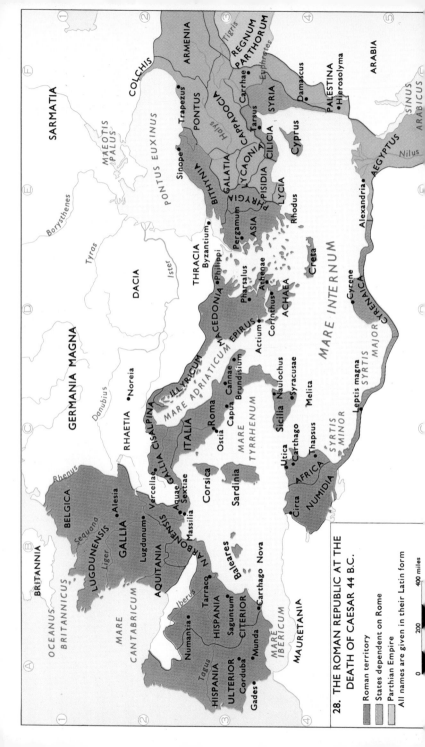

28. THE ROMAN REPUBLIC AT THE DEATH OF CAESAR 44 B.C.

- Roman territory
- States dependent on Rome
- Parthian Empire

All names are given in their Latin form

0   200   400 miles

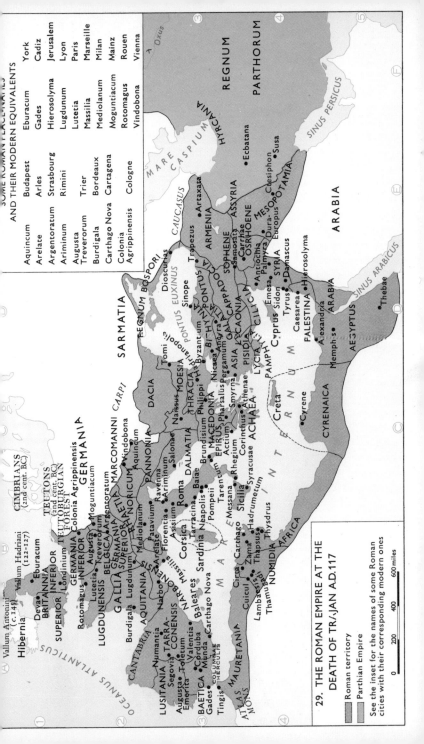

SOME ROMAN PLACE NAMES
AND THEIR MODERN EQUIVALENTS

Aquincum	Budapest	Eburacum	York
Arelate	Arles	Gades	Cadiz
Argentoratum	Strasbourg	Hierosolyma	Jerusalem
Ariminum	Rimini	Lugdunum	Lyon
Augusta Treverorum	Trier	Lutetia	Paris
Burdigala	Bordeaux	Massilia	Marseille
Carthago Nova	Cartagena	Mediolanum	Milan
Colonia Agrippinensis	Cologne	Moguntiacum	Mainz
		Rotomagus	Rouen
		Vindobona	Vienna

29. THE ROMAN EMPIRE AT THE DEATH OF TR/JAN A.D.117

■ Roman territory
□ Parthian Empire

See the inset for the names of some Roman cities with their corresponding modern ones

0 200 400 600 miles

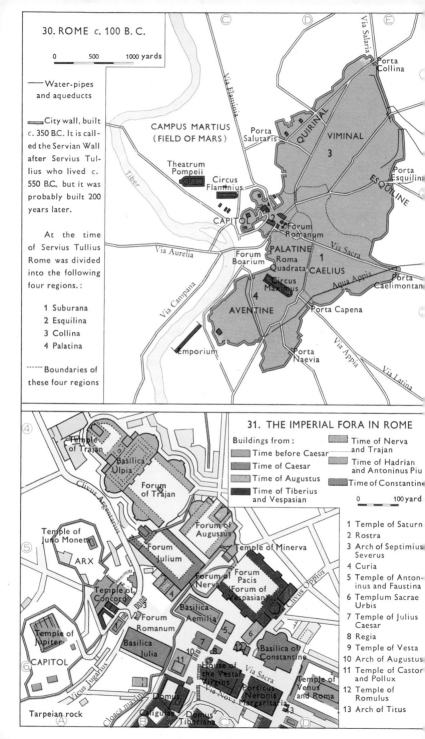

30. ROME c. 100 B.C.

0   500   1000 yards

— Water-pipes and aqueducts

— City wall, built c. 350 B.C. It is called the Servian Wall after Servius Tullius who lived c. 550 B.C., but it was probably built 200 years later.

At the time of Servius Tullius Rome was divided into the following four regions.:

1 Suburana
2 Esquilina
3 Collina
4 Palatina

------ Boundaries of these four regions

CAMPUS MARTIUS (FIELD OF MARS)

Via Flaminia
Via Salaria
Porta Collina
Porta Salutaris
QUIRINAL
VIMINAL
3
Theatrum Pompeii
Circus Flaminius
Porta Esquilina
ESQUILINE
Tiber
CAPITOL
Forum Romanum
Via Sacra
Via Aurelia
Forum Boarium
PALATINE
Roma Quadrata
1
CAELIUS
Aqua Appia
Porta Caelimontana
Via Canapana
Circus Maximus
4
AVENTINE
Porta Capena
Emporium
Porta Naevia
Via Appia
Via Latina

31. THE IMPERIAL FORA IN ROME

Buildings from:
Time before Caesar
Time of Caesar
Time of Augustus
Time of Tiberius and Vespasian
Time of Nerva and Trajan
Time of Hadrian and Antoninus Piu
Time of Constantin

0   100 yard

1 Temple of Saturn
2 Rostra
3 Arch of Septimius Severus
4 Curia
5 Temple of Antoninus and Faustina
6 Templum Sacrae Urbis
7 Temple of Julius Caesar
8 Regia
9 Temple of Vesta
10 Arch of Augustus
11 Temple of Castor and Pollux
12 Temple of Romulus
13 Arch of Titus

Temple of Trajan
Basilica Ulpia
Forum of Trajan
Clivus Argentarius
Temple of Juno Moneta
ARX
Forum Julium
Forum of Augustus
Temple of Minerva
Forum of Nerva
Temple of Concord
Forum Pacis
Forum of Vespasian
Clivus Oppius
Temple of Jupiter
CAPITOL
Forum Romanum
Basilica Aemilia
Vicus Jugarius
Basilica Julia
House of the Vestal Virgins
Via Sacra
Basilica of Constantine
Temple of Venus and Roma
Tarpeian rock
Cloaca maxima
Domus Caligulae
Domus Tiberiana
Porticus Neronis Margaritaria
Temple of Romulus

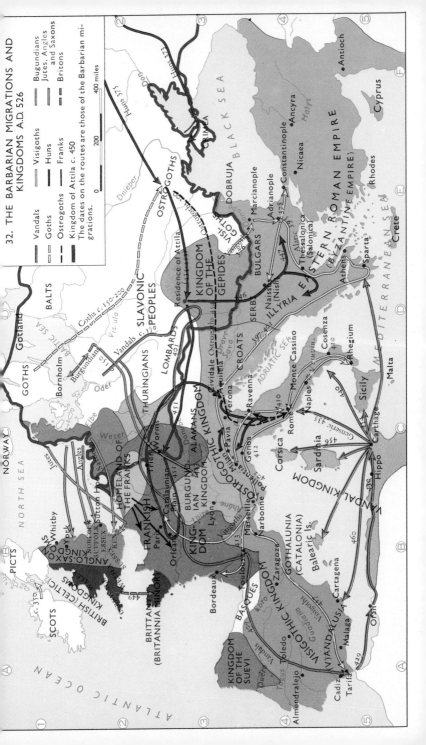

32. THE BARBARIAN MIGRATIONS AND KINGDOMS A.D. 526

Vandals — Burgundians, Jutes, Angles and Saxons
Goths
Visigoths
Huns — Britons
Ostrogoths
Franks
Kingdom of Attila c. 450

The dates on the routes are those of the Barbarian migrations.

0   200   400 miles

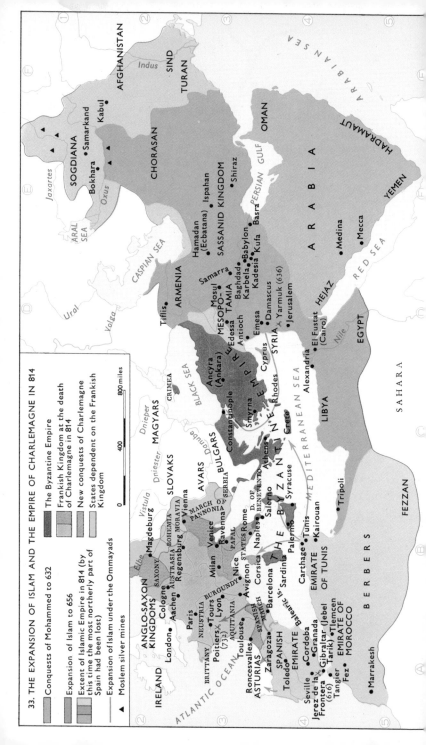

33. THE EXPANSION OF ISLAM AND THE EMPIRE OF CHARLEMAGNE IN 814

Conquests of Mohammed to 632

Expansion of Islam to 656

Expansion of Islam under the Ommayads

The Byzantine Empire

Frankish Kingdom at the death of Charlemagne in 814

New conquests of Charlemagne in 814

States dependent on the Frankish Kingdom

Extent of Islamic Empire in 814 (by this time the most northerly part of Spain had been lost)

▲ Moslem silver mines

0   400   800 miles

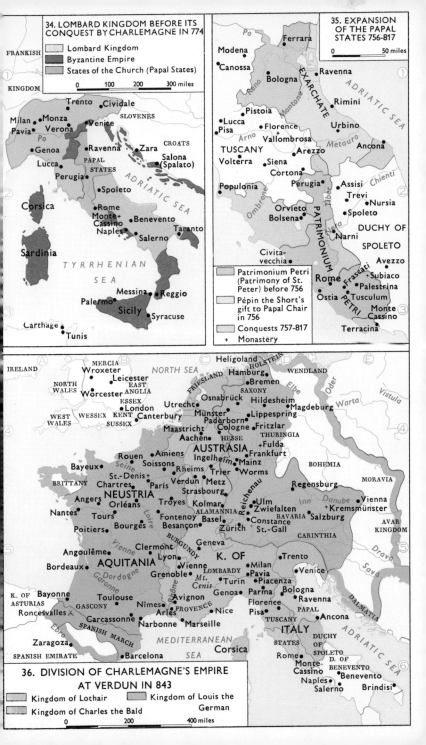

34. LOMBARD KINGDOM BEFORE ITS CONQUEST BY CHARLEMAGNE IN 774

- Lombard Kingdom
- Byzantine Empire
- States of the Church (Papal States)

0 100 200 300 miles

FRANKISH
KINGDOM

Trento · Cividale
Milan · Monza · Venice
Pavia · Verona
SLOVENES
Po
Genoa · Ravenna · Zara
Lucca · CROATS
Salona
(Spalato)
PAPAL
Perugia · STATES
ADRIATIC SEA
Spoleto
Corsica
Rome · Monte Benevento
Cassino · Taranto
Naples · Salerno

Sardinia

TYRRHENIAN SEA

Messina · Reggio
Palermo · Sicily
Carthage · Syracuse
Tunis

35. EXPANSION OF THE PAPAL STATES 756-817

0 50 miles

Po
Ferrara
Modena
Canossa
Bologna · Ravenna
EXARCHATE
Rimini
Pistoia
Lucca · Florence · Urbino
Pisa · Vallombrosa · Ancona
Arno · Arezzo · Metauro
TUSCANY
Volterra
Siena · Chienti
Populonia · Cortona · Assisi
Perugia · Trevi
Ombrone · Nursia
Orvieto · Spoleto
Bolsena · DUCHY OF
Narni · SPOLETO
Civita-vecchia · Avezzo
Tiber
PATRIMONIUM
Rome · Frascati · Subiaco
PETRI · Palestrina
Ostia · Tusculum
Monte
Cassino
Terracina

- Patrimonium Petri (Patrimony of St. Peter) before 756
- Pépin the Short's gift to Papal Chair in 756
- Conquests 757-817
- + Monastery

36. DIVISION OF CHARLEMAGNE'S EMPIRE AT VERDUN IN 843

- Kingdom of Lothair
- Kingdom of Charles the Bald
- Kingdom of Louis the German

0 200 400 miles

IRELAND
MERCIA · Heligoland
NORTH SEA · Hamburg · HOLSTEIN · WENDLAND
Wroxeter · Leicester · FRIESLAND · Bremen · Elbe · Oder · Vistula
NORTH WALES · East Anglia · SAXONY · Warta
Worcester · ESSEX · Osnabrück · Hildesheim · Magdeburg
WEST WALES · WESSEX · London · Utrecht · Münster · Paderborn · Lippspring · THURINGIA
KENT · Canterbury · Maastricht · Cologne · Fritzlar · BOHEMIA
SUSSEX · Aachen · HESSE · +Fulda
Rouen · Amiens · AUSTRASIA · Frankfurt · MORAVIA
Bayeux · Soissons · Ingelheim · Mainz
BRITTANY · St.-Denis · Rheims · Trier · Worms · Regensburg · Vienna
Chartres · Paris · Verdun · Metz · Danube · +Kremsmünster
Angers · NEUSTRIA · Troyes · Strasbourg · Reichenau · Ulm · Salzburg
Nantes · Orléans · Kolmar · ALAMANNIA · Zwiefalten · BAVARIA
Tours · Fontenoy · Basel · Constance · St.-Gall
Poitiers · Bourges · Besançon · Zürich · CARINTHIA
BURGUNDY · Geneva
Angoulême · Clermont · K. OF
AQUITANIA · Lyon · Vienne · Trento
Bordeaux · Grenoble · LOMBARDY · Milan · Venice
K. OF · Mt. · Pavia
ASTURIAS · Bayonne · GASCONY · Toulouse · Cenis · Turin · Piacenza · DALMATIA
Roncesvalles · Avignon · Genoa · Parma
Nîmes · PROVENCE · Florence · Bologna
Zaragoza · Carcassonne · Arles · Nice · Pisa · Ravenna
Narbonne · Marseille · TUSCANY · PAPAL · Ancona
SPANISH MARCH · Barcelona · MEDITERRANEAN · Corsica · ITALY · STATES
SPANISH EMIRATE · SEA · DUCHY OF
Rome · SPOLETO · D. OF
Monte- · BENEVENTO
Cassino · Benevento · Brindisi
Naples · Salerno

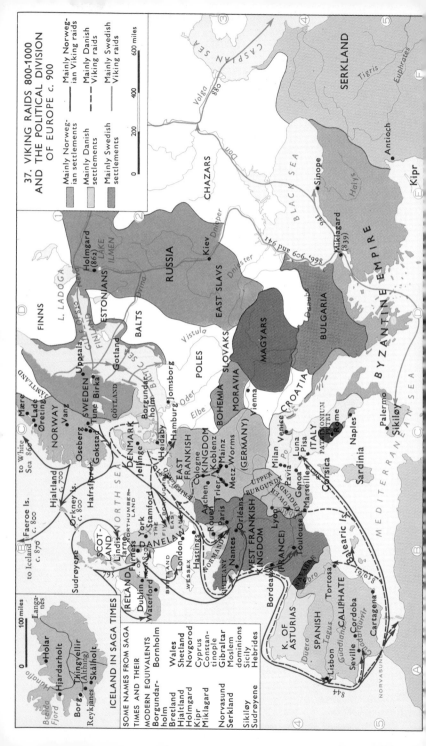

37. VIKING RAIDS 800–1000 AND THE POLITICAL DIVISION OF EUROPE c. 900

Mainly Norwegian settlements	—— Mainly Norwegian Viking raids
Mainly Danish settlements	- - - Mainly Danish Viking raids
Mainly Swedish settlements	—— Mainly Swedish Viking raids

0   200   400   600 miles

ICELAND IN SAGA TIMES

100 miles
0

Langanes

Breiða Fjord

Borg
Reykjanes
Þingvellir (Alþing)
Skálholt
Hjarðarholt
Hólar

Hunaflói

SOME NAMES FROM SAGA TIMES AND THEIR MODERN EQUIVALENTS

Borgundarholm — Bornholm
Bretland — Wales
Hjaltland — Shetland
Holmgard — Novgorod
Kipr — Cyprus
Miklagard — Constantinople
Norvasund — Gibraltar
Serkland — Moslem dominions
Sikiløy — Sicily
Sudrøyene — Hebrides

---

to White Sea 860

Mære
Lade
Oreting
Vang
Hjaltland
Faeroe Is. c. 800
to Iceland c. 870

NORWAY
Oseberg
Gokstad
Tune
Hafrsfjord
Uppsala
Birka
SWEDEN
JÄMTLAND
Gotland
GÖTLAND
Borgundarholm
Jomsborg

Orkney Is. c. 800
SCOT-LAND
Sudreyene
IRELAND
Dublin
Waterford
York
Lindisfarne
NORTHUMBER-LAND
THE FIVE BOROUGHS
DANELAW
Stamford
London
WESSEX
Bretland
79 I

Hedeby
Jellinge
DENMARK
NORTH SEA
Hamburg
BALTIC SEA
ESTONIANS
BALTS
FINNS
L. LADOGA
GULF OF FINLAND
Holmgard (862)
LAKE ILMEN
Neva

EAST FRANKISH KINGDOM (GERMANY)
Cologne
Aachen
Mainz
Trier
Koblenz
Metz
Worms
Bohemia
Moravia
Vienna
POLES
Oder
Elbe
Vistula

Rouen
NORMANDY
Paris
Orléans
BRITTANY
Nantes
WEST FRANKISH KINGDOM (FRANCE)
Hastings
UPPER BURGUNDY
LOWER BURGUNDY
Lyon
Marseille
Milan
Venice
Genoa
Luna
Pisa
Pavia
Po
ITALY
Rome
Naples
Palermo
Sikiløy
Sardinia
Corsica
CROATIA
SLOVAKS
MAGYARS
BULGARIA
Danube

Bordeaux
Toulouse
NAVARRE
Ebro
Tortosa
Cartagena
Balearic Is.
916/8
844
NORVASUND
K. OF ASTURIAS
Duero
Tagus
Lisbon
Seville
Cordoba
Guadalquivir
Guadiana
SPANISH CALIPHATE

MEDITERRANEAN SEA

RUSSIA
EAST SLAVS
Kiev
Dnieper
Dniester
Vistula
Don
Volga
880
CHAZARS
BLACK SEA
906 and 941
998
Miklagard (839)
Sinope
946
Halys
BYZANTINE EMPIRE
Antioch
Kipr
SERKLAND
Tigris
Euphrates
CASPIAN SEA

PRUSSIA

NORTH SEA

POMERANIA

• Jomsborg

Lübeck • MARCH OF THE BILLUNGS

• Hamburg

Bremen •

NORDMARK

FRIESLAND

Weser

Elbe

Oder

Rhine

DUCHY OF SAXONY

DUCHY OF POLAND

Hildesheim • • Magdeburg MARCH

Hameln • • Goslar OF LUSATIA

Corvey + Harzburg

Breslau •

Unstrut 933 Merseburg

Kaiserswerth MARCH OF MEISSEN

Antwerp • Cologne • Fritzlar THURINGIA Naumburg •

DUCHY OF Marburg HESSE Erfurt

Aachen Koblenz • Fulda + MARCH

LOWER LORRAINE D. OF FRANCONIA OF ZEITZ

Prague •

BOHEMIA

MORAVIA

Rheims • Trier • Bingen • Mainz • Tribur 932 Bamberg •

Verdun • Ingelheim Worms • Nuremberg •

D. OF UPPER Trifels • Speyer •

K. OF Troyes • LORRAINE ALSACE Württemberg • Regensburg •

OSTMARK

Clairvaux • Strasbourg Augsburg • Freising •

FRANCE *Saône* Reichenau 937 Basel Constance • St.-Gall Lechfeld 955

D. OF SWABIA 960

D. OF BAVARIA

Vienna •

KINGDOM

D. OF 954 Cluny • *Brenner Pass* D. OF CARINTHIA OF HUNGARY

BURGUNDY Geneva •

Drava

Lyon •

Rhône

K. OF BURGUNDY

Monza • VERONA

Milan • Venice •

LOMBARDY 899, 924 Mantua •

Mont Cenis Pavia • *Po*

KINGDOM

Turin • OF CROATIA

Avignon • Parma • Modena •

Canossa • Ravenna •

Arles • PROVENCE Genoa • Bologna •

K. OF

Marseille • K. OF ITALY PAPAL

SERBIA

Pisa • • Florence Ancona •

TUSCANY

Siena •

ADRIATIC SEA

Spoleto •

STATES

Corsica *Soracte* ✳ D. OF SPOLETO

Rome •

Lucera •

CAPUA APULIA

Sardinia Capua • BENEVENTO Castel del Monte (c. 1240)

Naples • Benevento • Brindisi •

Salerno • SALERNO Taranto •

TYRRHENIAN SEA

Cotrone •

38. THE HOLY ROMAN EMPIRE AND THE NORMAN KINGDOM IN SOUTH ITALY

▮ The Kingdom of Germany at the accession of Otto the Great in 936

▮ The Holy Roman Empire in 962, when Otto was crowned emperor

▮ Byzantine territories at end of 10th century

▮ Moslem territory at end of 10th century

→ Magyar raids in 10th century

━ Norman Kingdom in South Italy at the death of Roger II in 1154

Palermo • Messina •

Monreale • Cefalu •

Sicily Syracuse •

0   100   200   300 miles

K.

K. OF SCOTLAND

• Edinburgh

NORTH SEA

IRELAND
Dublin (Danish)•

Man

K. OF

• Durham
• Lancaster
York• ×Stamford

ENGLAND
Sherwood Forest

Norwich

• Worcester
Cardiff •Oxford

Exeter• Windsor •London Canterbury
Wight Hastings

Cork• •Waterford

WALES

ATLANTIC
OCEAN

Bremer

SAXON

•Utrecht

Münst

Cologne
•Aachen
Gelnhaus

C. OF FLANDERS
Bouvines
Amiens
Rouen

LORRAINE

Rhine
Maas

D. OF
Bayeux

D. OF BRITTANY

NORMANDY
Château-Gaillard
Chartres
Paris

Soissons

Rheims

Rüdeshei
Worms•
Trifels FRA
Weinsber

CHAMPAGNE
Sens

C. OF MAINE
C. OF ANJOU

Orléans

Strasbourg
Clairvaux
Waibling

KINGDOM OF

C. OF POITOU
Poitiers•

D. OF BURGUNDY

SWABIA

FRANCE

Cluny

K. OF

D. OF AQUITAINE
Clermont•

Geneva •
Lyon•

Bordeaux•

Legnano
Milan
Pavia
Piacenz
Roncagli
Genoa•

K. OF LEON

Oporto •
C. OF
PORTUGAL

Duero

D. OF GASCONY
K. OF NAVARRE
Toulouse

C. OF
TOULOUSE

BURGUNDY

Avignon
PROVENCE
Arles
Carcassonne •Marseille

•Nice

Burgos•

K. OF ARAGON

CASTILE

Zaragoza

Lerida
•Lerida

C. OF CATALONIA
(BARCELONA)

Corsica

Madrid•
•Toledo

•Barcelona

Tagus

Merida•

Valencia•

Balearic Is.

Sardinia

Seville•

Cordoba
•
Guadalquivir

Alicante•

MEDITERRA

Granada•
•Cadiz

•Cartagena

Tangier•
•Ceuta

CALIPHATE OF CORDOBA
DOMINIONS OF THE ALMORAVIDES

•Oran

Tunis

Guadiana

39. EUROPE IN 1100

- The Holy Roman Empire
- -- Kingdom of Canute 1028-35
- → William the Conqueror's invasion of England in 1066

For English possessions in France, see Map 50

0   100   200 miles

RWAY
slo

Uppsala
Dagö
ESTONIA
Ösel

K. OF
SWEDEN
Gotland

Kalmar Öland
LITHUANIA

Lund
BALTIC SEA
Memel

Bornholm

OF

NMARK

STEIN
MECKLEN-
BURG
POMERANIA
PRUSSIA

burg
Lüneburg

Brandenburg
RUSSIAN PRINCIPALITIES

Brunswick
Warta
Vistula

Kyffhäuser
K. OF POLAND

Vartburg
Breslau
Dnieper

Erfurt
nach
Main

Prague
Krakow

imberg
BOHEMIA

NIA
MORAVIA
Dniester
Bug

HOLY
Dürnstein

henstaufen
BAVARIA
Pressburg
Theiss
Prut

echfeld Salzburg
Vienna
CUMANS
(Turks)

ROMAN
Buda Pest

Merano
TRANSYL-
VANIA

EMPIRE
Drave
KINGDOM OF HUNGARY

scia
Venice
Sava
Danube

mona
VENICE
CROATIA

ossa

Bologna
Zara
Belgrade
BLACK SEA

OF Ravenna
Spalato
SERBIA

Florence
BULGARS

ITALY
Ragusa

Spoleto
Maritsa

APAL
Tiber
Adrianople

ATES Rome
Durazzo
Constantinople

Albano
Aquino
Thessalonica
Nicaea

D. OF
Bari

Naples APULIA
EPIRUS
BYZANTINE EMPIRE

Amalfi Salerno
Brindisi
Lesbos

Taranto

NORMAN
AEGEAN SEA

Cotrone
Ephesus

Athens

Messina
Corinth

Palermo
KINGDOM
Rhodes

C. OF
SICILY

Syracuse

AN

SEA
Crete

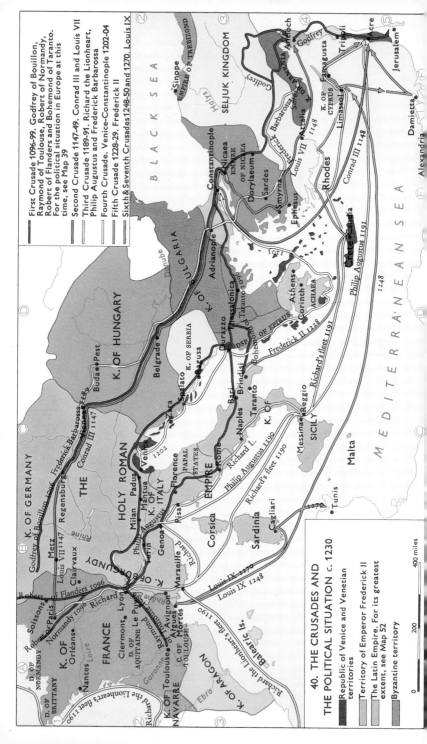

First Crusade 1096-99. Godfrey of Bouillon, Raymond of Toulouse, Robert of Normandy, Robert of Flanders and Bohemond of Taranto. For the political situation in Europe at this time, see Map 39

Second Crusade 1147-49. Conrad III and Louis VII

Third Crusade 1189-91. Richard the Lionheart, Philip Augustus and Frederick Barbarossa

Fourth Crusade. Venice-Constantinople 1202-04

Fifth Crusade 1228-29. Frederick II

Sixth & Seventh Crusades 1248-50 and 1270. Louis IX

40. THE CRUSADES AND THE POLITICAL SITUATION c. 1230

Republic of Venice and Venetian territories

Territory of Emperor Frederick II

The Latin Empire. For its greatest extent, see Map 52

Byzantine territory

0   200   400 miles

BLACK SEA

MEDITERRANEAN SEA

K. OF GERMANY

K. OF HUNGARY

THE HOLY ROMAN EMPIRE

SELJUK KINGDOM

EMPIRE OF TREBIZOND

EMPIRE OF NICAEA

K. OF SERBIA

K. OF BULGARIA

FRANCE

K. OF ITALY

PAPAL STATES

K. OF SICILY

K. OF NAVARRE

K. OF ARAGON

D. OF NORMANDY

D. OF BRITTANY

D. OF AQUITAINE

C. OF TOULOUSE

K. OF TOULOUSE

D. OF BURGUNDY

EMPIRE OF FERRUS

ACHAEA

K. OF CYPRUS

Corsica

Sardinia

Malta

Balearic Is.

Regensburg

Metz

Clairvaux

Soissons

Paris

Orléans

Nantes

Clermont

Le Puy

Lyon

Avignon

Aigues

Marseille

Genoa

Pisa

Florence

Milan

Padua

Mantua

Venice

Rome

Naples

Taranto

Bari

Brindisi

Reggio

Messina

Cagliari

Tunis

Buda

Pest

Belgrade

Zara

Spalato

Ragusa

Durazzo

Thessalonica

Adrianople

Constantinople

Nicaea

Dorylaeum

Sardes

Smyrna

Ephesus

Sinope

Attalia

Rhodes

Limassol

Famagusta

Antioch

Tripoli

Acre

Jerusalem

Damietta

Alexandria

Athens

Corinth

Godfrey of Bouillon 1096

Louis VII 1147

Conrad III 1147

Frederick Barbarossa 1189

Louis VII 1148

Conrad III 1148

Frederick 1189

Frederick II 1238

Philip Augustus 1191

Richard the Lionheart 1191

Richard's fleet 1190

Philip Augustus 1190

Richard L.

Louis IX 1270

Louis IX 1248

Robert of Normandy 1096

Robert of Flanders 1096

Bohemond of Taranto 1096

Richard the Lionheart's fleet 1190

1202

1921

Rhine

Loire

Garonne

Rhône

Ebro

Danube

Halys

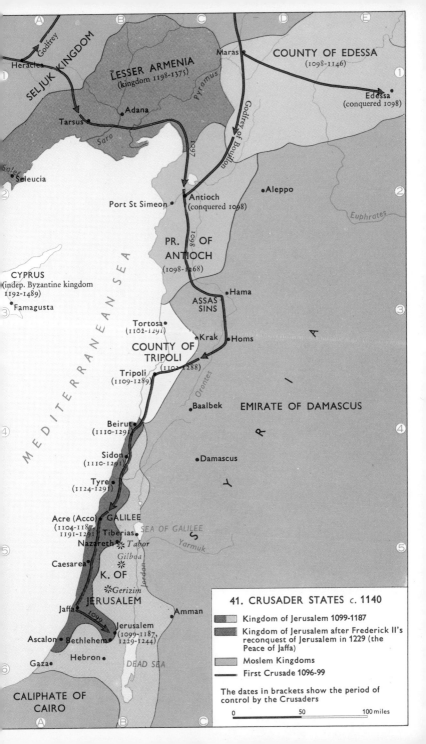

41. CRUSADER STATES c. 1140

Kingdom of Jerusalem 1099-1187

Kingdom of Jerusalem after Frederick II's reconquest of Jerusalem in 1229 (the Peace of Jaffa)

Moslem Kingdoms

First Crusade 1096-99

The dates in brackets show the period of control by the Crusaders

0   50   100 miles

Map labels

SELJUK KINGDOM

Godfrey

Heracles

LESSER ARMENIA
(kingdom 1198-1375)

Adana

Tarsus

Saro

Calet

Seleucia

Maras

COUNTY OF EDESSA
(1098-1146)

Edessa
(conquered 1098)

Pyramus

Godfrey of Bouillon

1097

Aleppo

Euphrates

Port St Simeon

Antioch
(conquered 1098)

PR. OF ANTIOCH
(1098-1268)

1098

CYPRUS
(indep. Byzantine kingdom
1192-1489)

Famagusta

MEDITERRANEAN SEA

Hama

ASSAS SINS

Tortosa
(1102-1291)

Krak

Homs

COUNTY OF TRIPOLI
(1102-1288)

Tripoli
(1109-1289)

Orontes

Baalbek

EMIRATE OF DAMASCUS

Beirut
(1110-1291)

Sidon
(1110-1291)

Damascus

Tyre
(1124-1291)

S   Y   R   I   A

Acre (Acco)
(1104-1187,
1191-1291)

GALILEE

Tiberias

SEA OF GALILEE

Yarmuk

Nazareth   Tabor

Caesarea

Gilboa

Jordan

K. OF

Gerizim

JERUSALEM

Jaffa

1099

Amman

Jerusalem
(1099-1187,
1229-1244)

Ascalon   Bethlehem

Gaza   Hebron

DEAD SEA

CALIPHATE OF CAIRO

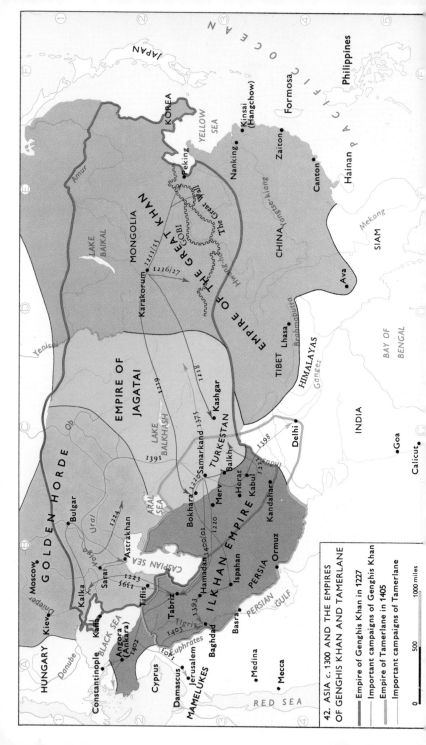

42. ASIA c. 1300 AND THE EMPIRES OF GENGHIS KHAN AND TAMERLANE

Empire of Genghis Khan in 1227
Important campaigns of Genghis Khan
Empire of Tamerlane in 1405
Important campaigns of Tamerlane

0   500   1000 miles

GOLDEN HORDE

EMPIRE OF JAGATAI

EMPIRE OF THE GREAT KHAN

ILKHAN EMPIRE

MONGOLIA

Karakorum   1211/15

1226/27

The Great Wall

GOBI

LAKE BAIKAL

Amur

JAPAN

KOREA

Peking

YELLOW SEA

Nanking   Kinsai (Hangchow)

Zaiton

Canton

Formosa

Hainan

Philippines

PACIFIC OCEAN

CHINA

Yangtse-kiang

Mekong

SIAM

Ava

TIBET   Lhasa

Brahmaputra

HIMALAYAS

Ganges

INDIA

BAY OF BENGAL

Goa

Calicut

Delhi

1398

TURKESTAN

Kashgar

1218

1219

Samarkand   1175

Bokhara   1220

Balkh

Merv

Herat   Kabul

Kandahar

PERSIA

Ispahan

Ormuz

Basra

PERSIAN GULF

Baghdad

Hamadan   1400/01

Tabriz

1393

1403

Tigris

Euphrates

Medina

Mecca

RED SEA

Damascus

Jerusalem

Cyprus

MAMELUKES

Constantinople

BLACK SEA

Angora (Ankara)   1402

Tiflis

1223

1395

Kaffa

Kiev

Moscow

HUNGARY

Danube

Dnieper

Bulgar

Ural

1224

Sarai

Astrakhan

CASPIAN SEA

Kalka

ARAL SEA

LAKE BALKHASH

1391

Ob

Yenisei

Volga

Kabul   1221

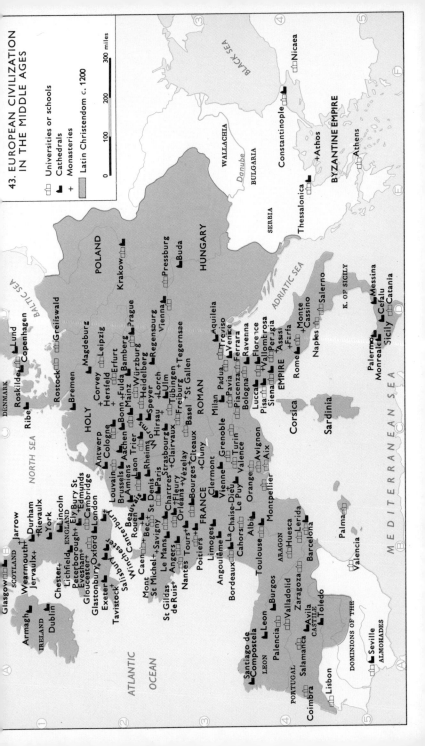

43. EUROPEAN CIVILIZATION IN THE MIDDLE AGES

- ⌂ Universities or schools
- ◣ Cathedrals
- + Monasteries
- ▨ Latin Christendom c. 1200

0 100 200 300 miles

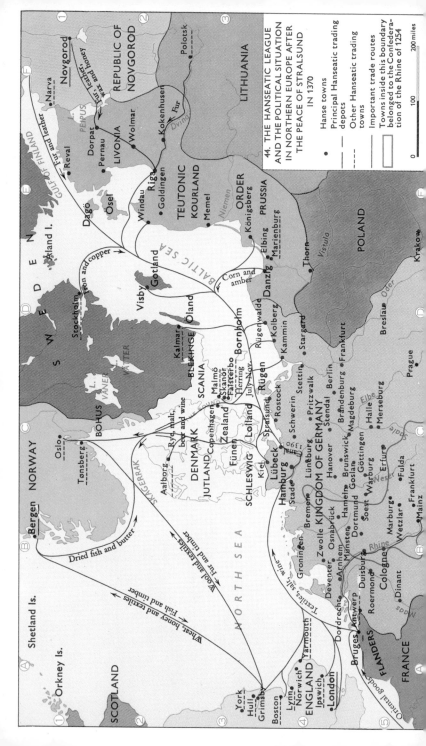

44. THE HANSEATIC LEAGUE AND THE POLITICAL SITUATION IN NORTHERN EUROPE AFTER THE PEACE OF STRALSUND IN 1370

- Hanse towns
- Principal Hanseatic trading depots
- Other Hanseatic trading towns
- Important trade routes
- Towns inside this boundary belonged to the Confederation of the Rhine of 1254

0   100   200 miles

Orkney Is.

Shetland Is.

SCOTLAND

York
Hull
Grimsby
Boston
Lynn
Norwich
Ipswich
ENGLAND
London

NORTH SEA

Wheat, honey and textiles

Fish and timber

Wool and textiles

Dried fish and butter

Bergen

NORWAY

Oslo
Tønsberg

BOHUS

SKAGERRAK

Aalborg
JUTLAND
DENMARK
Copenhagen
Zealand
Fünen
SCHLESWIG

S   W   E   D   E   N

L. VÄNER
L. VÄTTER

Stockholm

Iron and copper

Åland Is.

GULF OF FINLAND

Fur and leather

Reval

Narva

Novgorod

REPUBLIC OF NOVGOROD

Fur, leather, wax and honey

Polotsk

LITHUANIA

Dagö
Ösel
Dorpat
Pernau
Wolmar
Windau
Goldingen
Riga
Kokenhusen

Fur

L. PEPUS

LIVONIA

Dvina

TEUTONIC KOURLAND ORDER PRUSSIA

Memel
Königsberg
Elbing
Marienburg
Thorn

Niemen

Vistula

POLAND

Kraków

Breslau

Oder

Frankfurt

Prague

Spree

Berlin
Brandenburg
Magdeburg
Halle
Merseburg

Elbe

Erfurt
Göttingen
Goslar
Warburg
Fulda
Marburg
Wetzlar
Frankfurt
Mainz

Rhine

Cologne
Dinant
Roermond
Duisburg
Dortmund
Soest
Hameln
Brunswick
Hanover
Lüneburg
Stendal
Pritzwalk
Schwerin
Brandenburg

Maas

Antwerp
Bruges
FLANDERS
FRANCE

Oriental goods

Textiles, salt, wine

Wool and textiles

Deventer
Zwolle
Arnhem
Groningen
Münster
Osnabrück
Bremen
Stade
Hamburg
KINGDOM OF GERMANY

Kiel
Lübeck
Rostock
Stralsund
Rügen
Rügenwalde
Kolberg
Kolberg
Kammin
Stargard
Stettin
Schwerin

BALTIC SEA

Corn and amber

Danzig

Gotland
Visby

Öland

Bornholm

Falsterbo
Skanör
Malmö
SCANIA
BLEKINGE
Kalmar

Herring
July–Nov.

Lolland

Rye, malt, beer and wine

battle 1390

45. RENAISSANCE ITALY

Boundaries after the Peace of Lodi, 1454

0   50   100 miles

46. ACTIVITIES OF THE MEDICI AND FUGGERS IN WESTERN AND CENTRAL EUROPE c. 1500

● The Medici city (Florence) and branches

● The Fugger city (Augsburg) and branches

⚒ Fugger mines and iron-works

Most important commercial routes of the Medici

Most important commercial routes of the Fuggers

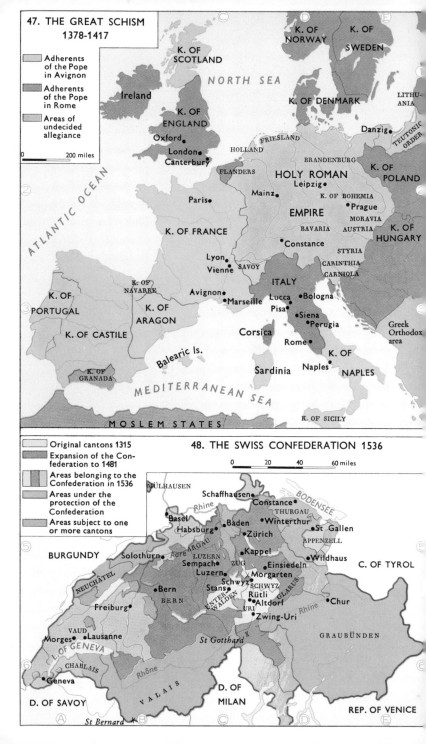

47. THE GREAT SCHISM 1378-1417

Adherents of the Pope in Avignon

Adherents of the Pope in Rome

Areas of undecided allegiance

0   200 miles

K. OF SCOTLAND

K. OF NORWAY

K. OF SWEDEN

NORTH SEA

Ireland

K. OF DENMARK

LITHU-ANIA

ATLANTIC OCEAN

K. OF ENGLAND

Oxford

London

Canterbury

FRIESLAND

HOLLAND

FLANDERS

Danzig

TEUTONIC ORDER

BRANDENBURG

K. OF POLAND

Paris

Mainz

HOLY ROMAN EMPIRE

Leipzig

K. OF BOHEMIA

Prague

MORAVIA

AUSTRIA

K. OF FRANCE

Constance

BAVARIA

STYRIA

CARINTHIA

CARNIOLA

K. OF HUNGARY

Lyon

Vienne

SAVOY

ITALY

Avignon

Marseille

Lucca

Pisa

Bologna

Siena

Perugia

Greek Orthodox area

K. OF NAVARRE

K. OF ARAGON

Corsica

Rome

K. OF PORTUGAL

K. OF CASTILE

Balearic Is.

Sardinia

Naples

K. OF NAPLES

K. OF GRANADA

MEDITERRANEAN SEA

MOSLEM STATES

K. OF SICILY

48. THE SWISS CONFEDERATION 1536

Original cantons 1315

Expansion of the Confederation to 1481

Areas belonging to the Confederation in 1536

Areas under the protection of the Confederation

Areas subject to one or more cantons

0   20   40   60 miles

MÜLHAUSEN

Schaffhausen

Constance

BODENSEE

THURGAU

Basel

Rhine

Habsburg

Baden

Winterthur

St Gallen

Aare

ARGAU

Zürich

APPENZELL

BURGUNDY

Solothurn

LUZERN

Kappel

Wildhaus

NEUCHÂTEL

Sempach

ZUG

Einsiedeln

C. OF TYROL

Luzern

Morgarten

Bern

Schwyz

SCHWYZ

Stans

UNTER WALDEN

Rütli

GLARUS

Chur

BERN

Altdorf

URI

Freiburg

Zwing-Uri

VAUD

Rhine

Morges

Lausanne

St Gotthard

GRAUBÜNDEN

L. OF GENEVA

CHABLAIS

Rhône

VALAIS

Geneva

D. OF SAVOY

St Bernard

D. OF MILAN

REP. OF VENICE

‡ AIX Archbishopric   • Bishopric

Areas directly under the Pope

The other tints serve to delineate the different archbishoprics. There is no significance in the fact that several areas are shown in the same tint

0   100   200   300 miles

NORTH SEA

BAY OF BISCAY

OTTOMAN EMPIRE

(to Lemberg)
(to Gnesen)
(to Kalocsa)

Places:

Trim, ‡DUBLIN, Leighlin, Ferns, ‡CASHEL, Waterford, St Asaph, Chester, Lincoln, Bangor, Lichfield, ‡YORK, Norwich, Coventry, Worcester, Ely, St Davids, Hereford, Llandaff, Bath, Wells, Salisbury, London, Rochester, Chichester, Winchester, Exeter

Lübeck, Ratzeburg, Schwerin, Havelberg, Brandenburg, HAMBURG‡, ‡BREMEN, Verden, Minden, Hildesheim, MAGDEBURG, Halberstadt, Paderborn, Merseburg, Naumburg, Meissen, Osnabrück, Münster, Utrecht, Liège, COLOGNE, Bamberg, Würzburg, Worms, Speyer, Strasbourg, Eichstätt, Augsburg, Freising, Regensburg, Passau, Wiener Neustadt, Chiemsee, ‡SALZBURG, Seckau, Gurk, Lavant, Brixen, Chur, Constance, Basel, Lausanne, Sitten, Geneva, TRIER‡, MAINZ‡, Metz, Verdun, Toul

PRAGUE, Olmütz, Vienna, Györ (Raab), ‡ESZTERGOM (GRAN), Neutra, Waitzen, Veszprem, ‡KALOCSA, Pécs (Fünfkirchen), Djakowo, Eger (Erlau), Oradea Mare (Grosswardein), Csanad, Agram, Laibach, Trieste, Pisino, Pola, Senj, Modrusch, ZARA, Senj, Ossero, Trau, Phar, SPALATO, Sebenico, Curzola, Almissa, Macarsa, Stagno Trebinje, Resino, RAGUSA‡, Sarajevo

AQUILEIA‡, Feltre, Belluno, Trento, Verona, Bergamo, Brescia, VENICE, Adria, Comacchio, Ferrara, RAVENNA‡, Faenza, Forlì, Rimini, Pesaro, Ancona, Fermo, Ascoli, Foligno, Assisi, Perugia, Arezzo, FLORENCE‡, SIENA, PISA‡, Lucca, Bobbio, Reggio, Parma, Piacenza, Pavia, Lodi, Como, MILAN, Novara, Vercelli, Ivrea, Aosta, Turin, Asti, Acqui, Alba, Savona, GENOA, Noli, Albenga, Ventimiglia, Mondovì, Nice, Grasse, Glandève, Fréjus, Toulon, Marseille

Thérouanne, Tournai, Cambrai, Arras, Amiens, Noyon, Laon, Soissons, Beauvais, Senlis, Meaux, Paris, RHEIMS, Châlons, Troyes, SENS‡, Chartres, Orléans, Auxerre, Langres, Autun, Chalon, Mâcon, BESANÇON‡, Mézières, Mende, MOUTIERS, Tarentaise, ‡LYON, VIENNE‡, Grenoble, Die, Valence, Le Puy, Gap, EMBRUN‡, Digne, Sisteron, Apt, ARLES‡, AVIGNON‡, St Pons, Alais, Montpellier, Uzès, ‡AIX, Béziers, NARBONNE‡, Carcassonne, Alet

ROUEN, Lisieux, Bayeux, Évreux, Sées, Coutances, Avranches, Trégnier, St Pol de Léon, St Malo, St Brieuc, Dol, Quimper, Vannes, Rennes, Nantes, Angers, Le Mans, TOURS‡, BOURGES‡, Nevers, Clermont, Limoges, Tulle, St Flour, Rodez, Sarlat, Cahors, Albi‡, Périgueux, Angoulême, Saintes, Poitiers, Luçon, Maillezais, Agen, Condom, AUCH‡, TOULOUSE‡, Pamiers, St Bertrand, Lescar, Oloron, Dax, Aire, Bazas, BORDEAUX‡, Bayonne, Pamplona, Rennes

‡YORK, CANTERBURY, ROUEN, SENS, RHEIMS, TRIER, MAINZ, COLOGNE, BREMEN, MAGDEBURG, PRAGUE, SALZBURG, BESANÇON, LYON, VIENNE, EMBRUN, ARLES, AIX, AVIGNON, NARBONNE, TOULOUSE, AUCH, BORDEAUX, BOURGES, TOURS, GENOA, MILAN, AQUILEIA, VENICE, RAVENNA, FLORENCE, PISA, SIENA, SPALATO, ZARA, RAGUSA, KALOCSA, ESZTERGOM, BURGOS‡

Elbe, Rhine, Danube

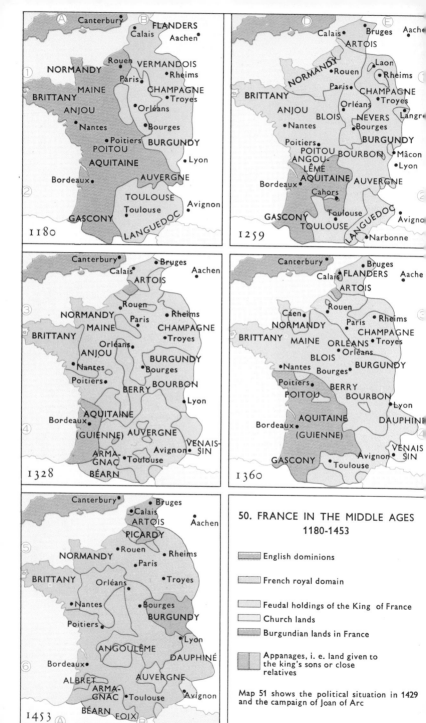

50. FRANCE IN THE MIDDLE AGES
1180-1453

- English dominions
- French royal domain
- Feudal holdings of the King of France
- Church lands
- Burgundian lands in France
- Appanages, i. e. land given to the king's sons or close relatives

Map 51 shows the political situation in 1429 and the campaign of Joan of Arc

1180 map:
Canterbury · FLANDERS · Calais · Aachen · NORMANDY · Rouen · VERMANDOIS · Paris · Rheims · MAINE · CHAMPAGNE · BRITTANY · ANJOU · Orléans · Troyes · Nantes · Bourges · Poitiers · BURGUNDY · POITOU · AQUITAINE · Lyon · Bordeaux · AUVERGNE · TOULOUSE · Avignon · Toulouse · GASCONY · LANGUEDOC

1259 map:
Calais · Bruges · Aache · ARTOIS · NORMANDY · Laon · Rouen · Rheims · Paris · BRITTANY · CHAMPAGNE · ANJOU · Orléans · Troyes · BLOIS · NEVERS · Langre · Nantes · Bourges · Poitiers · BURGUNDY · POITOU · BOURBON · Mâcon · ANGOU-LÊME · Lyon · AQUITAINE · AUVERGNE · Bordeaux · Cahors · GASCONY · Toulouse · LANGUEDOC · Avigno · TOULOUSE · Narbonne

1328 map:
Canterbury · Bruges · Calais · Aachen · ARTOIS · Rouen · NORMANDY · Paris · Rheims · MAINE · CHAMPAGNE · BRITTANY · Orléans · Troyes · ANJOU · Nantes · BURGUNDY · Poitiers · Bourges · BERRY · BOURBON · Lyon · AQUITAINE · (GUIENNE) · AUVERGNE · Bordeaux · VENAIS-SIN · ARMA-GNAC · Avignon · Toulouse · BÉARN

1360 map:
Canterbury · Bruges · Calais · Aache · FLANDERS · ARTOIS · Caen · Rouen · NORMANDY · Paris · Rheims · BRITTANY · MAINE · ORLÉANS · CHAMPAGNE · Orléans · Troyes · BLOIS · BURGUNDY · Nantes · Bourges · Poitiers · BERRY · BOURBON · POITOU · Lyon · DAUPHINÉ · AQUITAINE · (GUIENNE) · Bordeaux · VENAIS-SIN · GASCONY · Avignon · Toulouse

1453 map:
Canterbury · Bruges · Calais · ARTOIS · PICARDY · Aachen · NORMANDY · Rouen · Rheims · Paris · BRITTANY · Orléans · Troyes · Nantes · Bourges · BURGUNDY · Poitiers · Lyon · ANGOULÊME · DAUPHINÉ · Bordeaux · AUVERGNE · ALBRET · Avignon · ARMA-GNAC · Toulouse · BÉARN · FOIX

51. ENGLAND AND FRANCE IN 1429

English possessions
Lands of the French crown
Feudal holdings of the French crown
Church lands
Burgundian lands
—— Joan of Arc's campaign

0   50   100   150   200 miles

ULSTER

K. OF SCOTLAND

NORTHUMBERLAND

IRELAND

Man

Carlisle
CUMBERLAND
Richmond

Lancaster
LANCASTER
YORKSHIRE
York
Towton

Dublin

Conway
Wakefield
LINCOLN

K. OF ENGLAND

Shrewsbury
NOTTINGHAM
Nottingham
LEICESTER
Bosworth
NORFOLK
WARWICK
Kenilworth
Ely
WOR-
CESTER
Warwick
WALES
HEREFORD
GLOU-
Cambridge
Gloucester
BED-
FORD
SUFFOLK
CESTER
HERTFORD
Berkeley
Bristol
Oxford
ESSEX
Bath
Windsor
London
SOMERSET
WILT-
SHIRE
Canterbury
DEVON
DORSET
HAMPSHIRE
SUSSEX
KENT
CORNWALL

NORTH SEA

ZEELAND
Blankenberghe
Sluys
HOLLAND
Rhine
Maas

Bruges
FLANDERS
Ghent
BRABANT

Calais
Ypres
ARTOIS
Lille
Brussels
Cologne
LIM-
BURG
Agincourt
Arras
Liège
Namur
Limburg
Crécy
PICARDY
HAINAULT
LUXEMBOURG

ENGLISH CHANNEL

Cherbourg
Amiens
Péronne

Harfleur
Rouen
Laon
RÉTHEL

Caen
Beauvais
VALOIS
Soissons
Rheims

NORMANDY
Compiègne
Marne
Châlons
Nancy
LORRAINE

ILE-DE-FRANCE
St Denis
CHAMPAGNE

BRITTANY
Paris
Seine
Domrémy

MAINE
Chartres
Brétigny
Montereau
Troyes

ANJOU
Patay
ORLÉANS
Sens

Nantes
Blois
Orléans
Auxerre

Plessis
Tours
Loire

Chinon
Amboise
NEVERS
Dijon

POITOU
Bourges
BERRY
Nevers
FRANCHE-
COMTÉ
Besançon

Poitiers
BOURBON
BURGUNDY

La Rochelle
Geneva

BAY OF BISCAY
Limoges
DUCHY OF SAVOY

Clermont
Lyon
Vienne

Blaye
Dordogne

AQUITAINE
AUVERGNE
Le Puy
DAUPHINÉ

Bordeaux
(GUIENNE)
Cahors

Rodez
Rhône

GASCONY
Albi
VENAISSIN

Bayonne
ARMAGNAC
Castres
Avignon

BÉARN
Toulouse
PROVENCE

K. OF NAVARRE
LANGUEDOC
Marseille

K. OF CASTILE
Narbonne
Toulon

Ebro

K. OF ARAGON
MEDITERRANEAN SEA

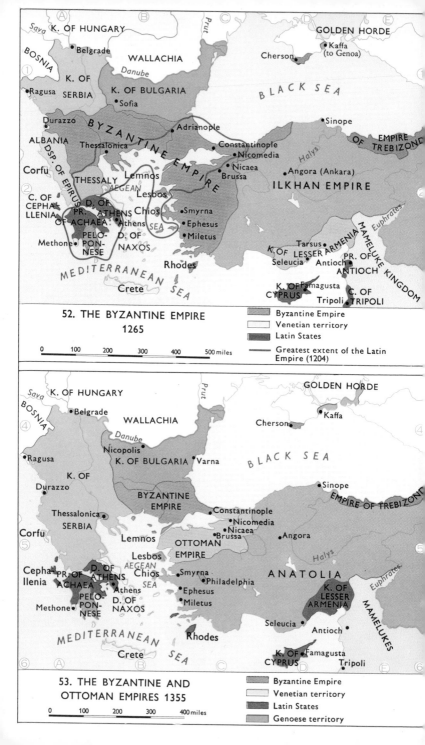

52. THE BYZANTINE EMPIRE 1265

	Byzantine Empire
	Venetian territory
	Latin States
	Greatest extent of the Latin Empire (1204)

0   100   200   300   400   500 miles

53. THE BYZANTINE AND OTTOMAN EMPIRES 1355

	Byzantine Empire
	Venetian territory
	Latin States
	Genoese territory

0   100   200   300   400 miles

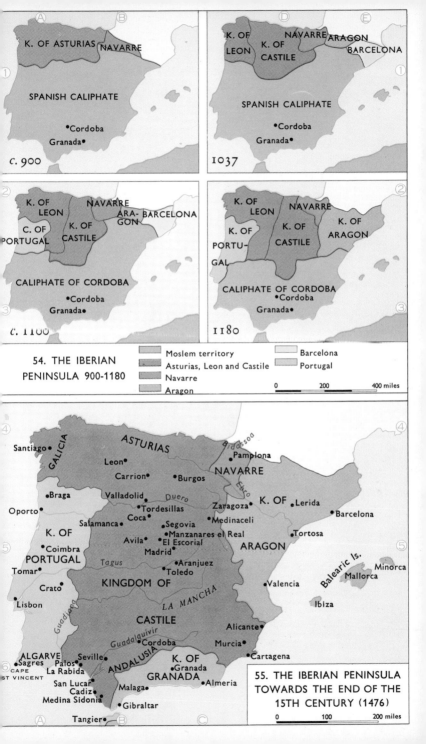

54. THE IBERIAN PENINSULA 900–1180

Moslem territory
Asturias, Leon and Castile
Navarre
Aragon
Barcelona
Portugal

0   200   400 miles

55. THE IBERIAN PENINSULA TOWARDS THE END OF THE 15TH CENTURY (1476)

0   100   200 miles

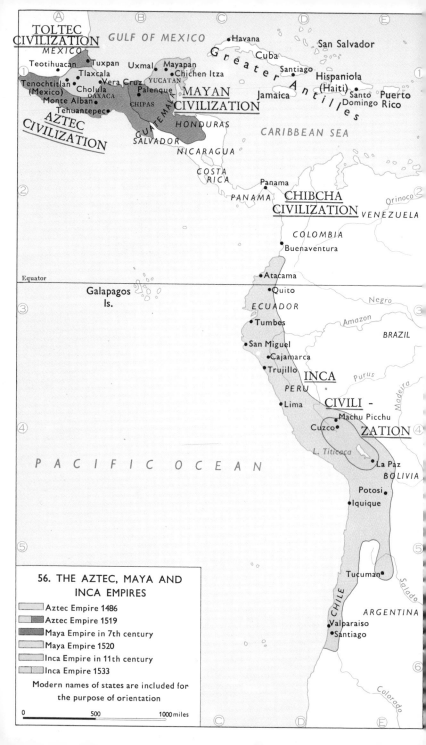

**56. THE AZTEC, MAYA AND
INCA EMPIRES**

- Aztec Empire 1486
- Aztec Empire 1519
- Maya Empire in 7th century
- Maya Empire 1520
- Inca Empire in 11th century
- Inca Empire 1533

Modern names of states are included for
the purpose of orientation

0 — 500 — 1000 miles

57. EUROPE IN 1556. THE HABSBURG DOMINIONS

- Inheritance of Charles V
- Philip II's part of the inheritance
- Ferdinand I's part of the inheritance
- The Ottoman Empire
- Republic of Venice and Venetian territory
- Boundary of the Holy Roman Empire

0   200   400 miles

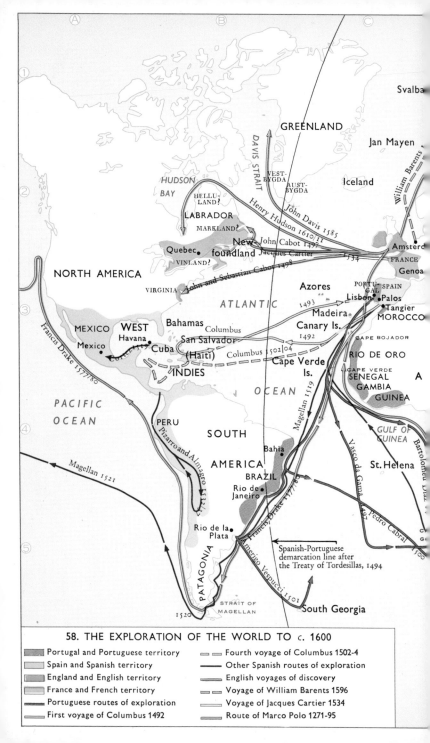

58. THE EXPLORATION OF THE WORLD TO c. 1600

▨ Portugal and Portuguese territory	═ ═ Fourth voyage of Columbus 1502-4
▨ Spain and Spanish territory	── Other Spanish routes of exploration
▨ England and English territory	═══ English voyages of discovery
▨ France and French territory	═ ═ Voyage of William Barents 1596
── Portuguese routes of exploration	═ ═ Voyage of Jacques Cartier 1534
═══ First voyage of Columbus 1492	═══ Route of Marco Polo 1271-95

Map labels:

Svalba
GREENLAND
Jan Mayen
Iceland
DAVIS STRAIT
VEST-BYGDA
AUST-BYGDA
HUDSON BAY
HELLU-LAND?
LABRADOR
MARKLAND?
William Barents
John Davis 1585
Henry Hudson 1610/11
Amsterd
FRANCE
Genoa
New-foundland
John Cabot 1497
Jacques Cartier 1534
Quebec
VINLAND?
NORTH AMERICA
VIRGINIA John and Sebastian Cabot 1498
Azores
PORTU-GAL SPAIN
Lisbon Palos
Tangier
MOROCCO
ATLANTIC
1493
Madeira
Bahamas Columbus
Canary Is.
1492
CAPE BOJADOR
MEXICO WEST
Havana
Mexico Cortez 1519
Cuba
San Salvador (Haiti)
Columbus 1502/04
Cape Verde Is.
RIO DE ORO
CAPE VERDE
SENEGAL
GAMBIA
GUINEA
A
INDIES
Francis Drake 1577/80
OCEAN
Magellan 1519
PACIFIC OCEAN
PERU
Pizarro and Almagro 1531/34
SOUTH AMERICA
BRAZIL
Bahia
Rio de Janeiro
GULF OF GUINEA
St. Helena
Vasco da Gama 1497/98
Bartolomeu Diaz
Magellan 1521
Rio de la Plata
Francis Drake 1577/80
Amerigo Vespucci 1501
Pedro Cabral
Spanish-Portuguese demarcation line after the Treaty of Tordesillas, 1494
PATAGONIA
STRAIT OF MAGELLAN
1520
South Georgia

ARCTIC OCEAN

BARENTS SEA

Steven Borough 1556

Richard Chancellor 1556

Novaya Zemlya

WHITE SEA

RUSSIA

A S I A

TARTARY

Karakorum

Constantinople

Samarkand

Peking

JAPAN (ZIPANGU)

Alexandria

EGYPT

PERSIA

Ormuz

Marco Polo 1271/95

TIBET

CHINA

PACIFIC OCEAN

ARABIA

Aden

INDIA

MALABAR

Goa

Calicut

Cochin

SIAM

Philippines

Mactan

Cebu

Ladrones

Magellan 1521

ETHIOPIA

Vasco da Gama 1498

COAST

Ceylon

EAST

Malacca

Carolines

Melinde

Pedro Cabral 1500

Borneo

Moluccas

Mombassa

INDIES

Celebes

New Guinea

Sumatra

Batavia Java

INDIAN OCEAN

Mozambique

Madagascar

Francis Drake 1577/80

NEW HOLLAND (AUSTRALIA)

Magellan's ship Victoria commanded by del Cano 1522

Tasmania
(discovered by
Abel J. Tasman
in 1642)

Spanish-Portuguese
demarcation line after
the Treaty of Zaragoza, 1529

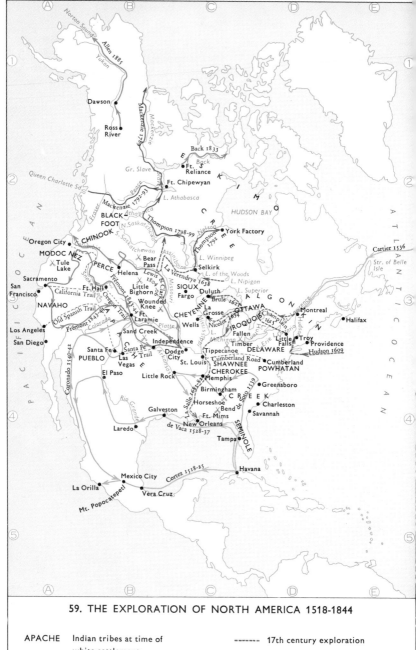

59. THE EXPLORATION OF NORTH AMERICA 1518-1844

APACHE   Indian tribes at time of
                white settlement

    ✗   Battlefields of Indian wars

           16th century exploration

---------   17th century exploration

—————   18th century exploration

—————   19th century exploration

0   200   400   600   800   1000 miles

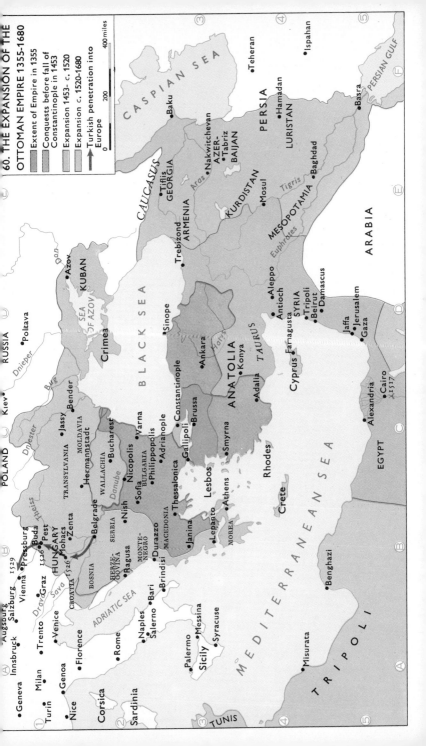

60. THE EXPANSION OF THE OTTOMAN EMPIRE 1355-1680

Extent of Empire in 1355
Conquests before fall of Constantinople in 1453
Expansion 1453 – c. 1520
Expansion c. 1520-1680
Turkish penetration into Europe

0   200   400miles

RUSSIA

•Poltava
•Kiev

POLAND

Dnieper

Don

Azov•

SEA OF AZOV

KUBAN

Bug

Dniester

Bender•

•Jassy

Crimea

BLACK SEA

MOLDAVIA

•Bucharest

Hermannstadt•

TRANSYLVANIA

WALLACHIA

Danube

•Nicopolis

Varna•

•Sinope

Sinope

•Ankara

ANATOLIA

•Konya

•Adalia

•Smyrna

Brussa•

Gallipoli

Constantinople

Adrianople•

•Philippopolis

BULGARIA

Sofia•

•Nish

Belgrade•

SERBIA

•Zenta

Mohacs 1526

Buda•

•Pest

HUNGARY

1526

Graz•

Pressburg•

Vienna• 1529

Salzburg•

•Augsburg

Innsbruck•

•Trento

Venice•

•Milan

•Genoa

•Florence

Turin•

Geneva•

Nice•

Corsica

Sardinia

•Rome

Naples•

•Salerno

Bari•

•Brindisi

Ragusa

BOSNIA

HERZE-GOVINA

MONTE-NEGRO

•Durazzo

Janina•

MACEDONIA

•Thessalonica

•Lepanto

MOREA

Athens•

Lesbos

Rhodes

Crete

•Palermo

Sicily

•Messina

•Syracuse

MEDITERRANEAN SEA

•Benghazi

•Misurata

TRIPOLI

TUNIS

ADRIATIC SEA

Sava

Drava

Theiss

CROATIA 1526

Drava

CAUCASUS

•Tiflis

GEORGIA

ARMENIA

•Trebizond

Aras

Nakwitchevan•

AZER-BAIJAN

•Tabriz

•Baku

CASPIAN SEA

•Teheran

PERSIA

•Hamadan

LURISTAN

•Baghdad

Tigris

KURDISTAN

•Mosul

Euphrates

MESOPOTAMIA

•Basra

PERSIAN GULF

ARABIA

•Aleppo

•Antioch

SYRIA

•Damascus

•Beirut

•Tripoli

•Jaffa

•Jerusalem

•Gaza

Cyprus

Famagusta•

TAURUS

Halys

•Cairo 1517

Alexandria•

EGYPT

61. THE NETHERLANDS WAR OF INDEPENDENCE

Boundary of the northern provinces which, after the Union of Utrecht in 1579, formed the republic of the United Provinces

Catholic Union of Arras 1579

Spanish Netherlands

Church lands

Ghent — Names underlined indicate towns in the Spanish Netherlands which belonged temporarily to the Union of Utrecht

0   20   40   60 miles

62. FRANCE DURING THE HUGUENOT WARS 1562-92

K. OF ENGLAND
Fotheringhay
Kenninghall
Warwick

UNITED PROVINCES
Amsterdam
Rotterdam

London
Windsor
Dover
Southampton
Plymouth
Isle of Wight

Calais
Boulogne

FLANDERS
SPANISH
Brussels
Antwerp

Cologne
Siegen

B. OF LIÈGE

ENGLISH CHANNEL

Eu
Amiens
Arques 1589
St Quentin
Le Havre
Rouen
Condé
Cateau-Cambrésis
Peronne
Guise
Noyon
Mézières
Vervins

NETHERLANDS

Metz
HOLY
ROMAN
EMPIRE

NORMANDY
Seine
Poissy
St Denis
Ivry 1590
St Germain
Dreux 1562
Alençon

Rheims
Verdun
Toul

BRITTANY
Mayenne
MAINE

Meaux
Paris
Vassy

CHAMPAGNE

Nantes

ANJOU
Vendôme
Blois 1576, 1588
Amboise 1563
Tours

Fontainebleau
Orléans
Gien
Chambord

BURGUNDY
Dijon
FRANCHE-
COMTÉ
Besançon

POITOU
Chatellerault
Poitiers
BERRY
Loire
Bourges
Nevers
Moulins 1576
BOURBON

Luçon 1569
La Rochelle
LA MARCHE
Montpensier
Clermont

FOREZ

Geneva
Lyon
SAVOY

BAY OF BISCAY

Cognac
Jarnac 1569
Vienne
PÉRIGORD
Coutras 1587
Bordeaux
Bergerac
GUIENNE
Dordogne
Cahors
Garonne

Beaulieu
Murat
AUVERGNE
Carlat

Valence
DAUPHINÉ
Rhône
ORANGE
Avignon
Nîmes

PROVENCE
Marseille
Toulon

Bayonne
GASCONY
NAVARRE
BÉARN
Toulouse
LANGUEDOC
Montpellier
Narbonne
Foix

Loyola
Pamplona
NAVARRE

Andorra

K. OF SPAIN
Ebro
Huesca
Zaragoza
CATALONIA
Barcelona
Tarragona

MEDITERRANEAN SEA

Provinces loyal to the king
Huguenot areas
Provinces supporting the Guises
Spanish territory

0   100   200   300 miles

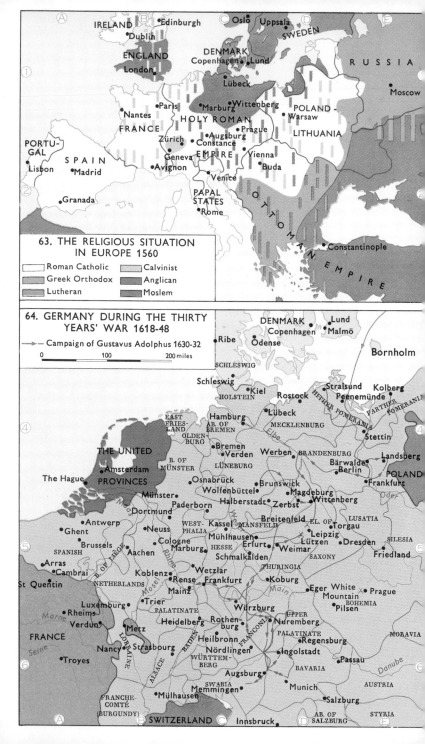

63. THE RELIGIOUS SITUATION IN EUROPE 1560

Roman Catholic
Greek Orthodox
Lutheran
Calvinist
Anglican
Moslem

64. GERMANY DURING THE THIRTY YEARS' WAR 1618-48

→ Campaign of Gustavus Adolphus 1630-32

0   100   200 miles

65. ENGLAND, SCOTLAND AND IRELAND IN THE MID-17TH CENTURY

Areas controlled by Charles I in 1642

Charles I's conquests 1643

Area controlled by Parliament in 1642

Conquests by Parliament in 1643

Area controlled by Parliament in 1645

Areas of Ireland where English and Scottish Protestants were settled during the time of Cromwell

Irish areas given to English settlers c. 1650

0   50   100 miles

THE EDINBURGH AREA

Dundee
MURRAY
FIRTH OF TAY
Kinross   St Andrews
LINDSAY
Loch Leven   FIRTH OF FORTH
Edinburgh   Leith
Craigmillar   Holyrood
Bothwell   Carberry Hill

Orkneys

Hebrides

Dunrobin

MORAY FIRTH

Inverness
MORAY   Aberdeen
Balmoral
Dalnaspidal
Glencoe   Killiecrankie
ANGUS
SCOTLAND
Perth   Dundee
Stirling
Dunbar
Glasgow   Edinburgh
Douglas
Ayr
Turnberry
Dumfries   NORTH-UMBERLAND
Carlisle   Newcastle
SOLWAY FIRTH   Durham
WEST-MORLAND

NORTH SEA

ATLANTIC OCEAN

Londonderry
TYRONE
ULSTER   Belfast

Man

IRISH SEA

YORKSHIRE
Lancaster   York
Preston   Leeds   Hull
LANCA-   Bradford
Manchester SHIRE   Gainsborough
Conway   CHESHIRE   Lincoln
Sheffield   NOTTINGHAM
Derby   Nottingham
Shrewsbury   LEICESTER   Norwich
Leicester   NORFOLK
ENGLAND   Ely   Cambridge
Naseby   SUFFOLK
Worcester   Stratford   Bedford   Harwich
Edgehill   ESSEX
Cardigan   Buckingham   Hatfield
Pembroke   Gloucester   Oxford   London
Berkeley   Reading   Greenwich
Castle   Bristol   Canterbury
Bath   Newbury   SURREY   KENT   Dover
Sedgemoor   Salisbury
Bridgwater   SOMERSET   SUSSEX
Taunton   Southampton   BEACHY HEAD
DEVON   DORSET   Isle of Wight
Plymouth   Tor Bay
CORNWALL

CONNAUGHT
Drogheda
Boyne
IRELAND   Dublin
LEINSTER
Limerick
Kilkenny
MUNSTER   Wexford
Cork

ENGLISH CHANNEL

66 LONDON c. 1600

0   ½   1   1½ miles

MIDDLESEX
Bethnal Green
Gray's Inn
Mile End   Bromley
Lincoln's Inn   WHITE   Stepney
CHAPEL
MAYFAIR   St Paul's
LONDON   CITY
HYDE PARK   London   Tower   Poplar
Bridge
Globe Theatre
Whitehall
WEST-   Westminster SOUTHWARK
Kensington   MINSTER
Buckingham   Abbey
Palace   Parliament   Lambeth
(built 1698)   Newington
Brompton   Vauxhall   Walworth
Chelsea   DEPTFORD   GREEN-WICH
Nine Elms   SURREY
Thames   Thames
A   B   C   D   E

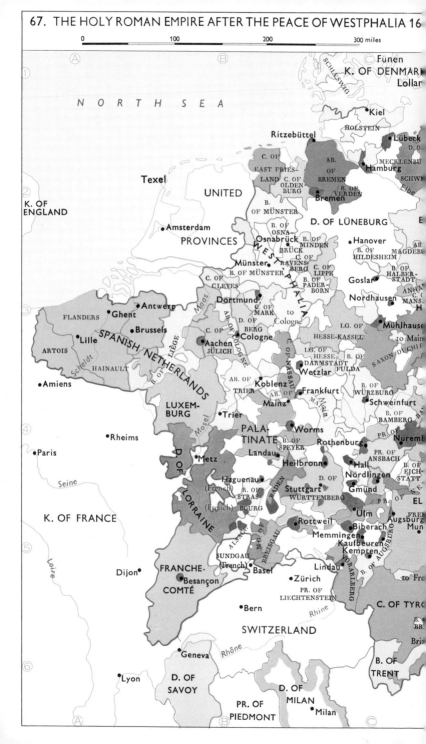

0   100   200   300 miles

Fünen
K. OF DENMAR
Lollar

NORTH SEA

SCHLESWIG

Kiel

HOLSTEIN

Ritzebüttel
Lübeck
D. O.
MECKLENBU
Hamburg
SCHW

C. OF
EAST FRIES-
LAND
C. OF
OLDEN-
BURG
AB.
OF
BREMEN
B. OF
VERDEN
Elbe

Texel

UNITED

Bremen

B. OF MÜNSTER

D. OF LÜNEBURG
E

K. OF
ENGLAND

Amsterdam

PROVINCES

B. OF
OSNA-
BRÜCK
Osnabrück B. OF
MINDEN
Hanover
AB
B. OF
MAGDEB
HILDESHEIM

WESTPHALIA

Münster
C. OF
RAVENS-
BERG
C. OF
LIPPE
B. OF
HALBER-
STADT

B. OF MÜNSTER
B. OF
PADER-
BORN
Goslar
ANH
C. C
MANS
H

C. OF
CLEVES
Dortmund
Nordhausen

Antwerp
C. OF
MARK
to
Cologne
LG. OF
Mühlhause
FLANDERS
Ghent
AB. OF
COLOGNE
D. OF
BERG
HESSE-KASSEL
to Main

SPANISH NETHERLANDS
Brussels
Lille
C. OF
JÜLICH
Cologne
Aachen
LG. OF
HESSE-
DARMSTADT
B. OF
FULDA
SAXON DUCHIE
ARTOIS
B. OF LIÈGE

HAINAULT
Wetzlar
C. OF NASSAU

Amiens
AB. OF
TRIER
Koblenz
Frankfurt
B. OF
WÜRZBURG
Schweinfurt
Mainz
MAIN

LUXEM-
BURG
Trier
PALA-
TINATE
Worms
Rothenburg
B. OF
BAMBERG
BAY
Nurem
D. OF LORRAINE
Metz
B. OF
SPEYER
Rothenburg
PR. OF
Paris
Landau
Heilbronn
PR. OF
ANSBACH
Rheims
Mosel
Haguenau
(French)
B. OF
STRAS-
BOURG
Hall
Nördlingen
B. OF
EICH-
STÄTT
Seine
D. OF
WÜRTTEMBERG
Stuttgart
Gmünd
PR. OF
EL

K. OF FRANCE
BADEN
Rottweil
Ulm
Augsburg
FRE
Mün
Biberach
Memmingen
Kaufbeuren
Kempten
B. OF
AUGSBUR
SUNDGAU
(French)
Basel
Lindau
to Fre
Dijon
FRANCHE-
COMTÉ
Besançon
PR. OF
LIECHTENSTEIN
VORARLBERG
Bern
Rhine
C. OF TYRO
Loire
SWITZERLAND
B.
BR
Geneva
Rhône
Bris
Lyon
D. OF
SAVOY
B. OF
TRENT
PR. OF
PIEDMONT
D. OF
MILAN
Milan

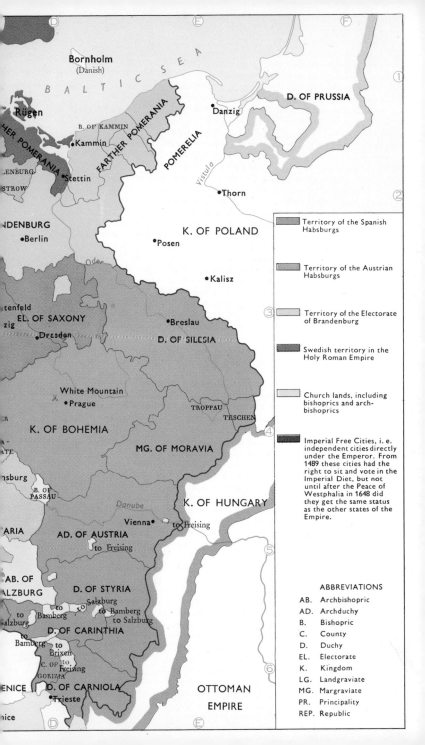

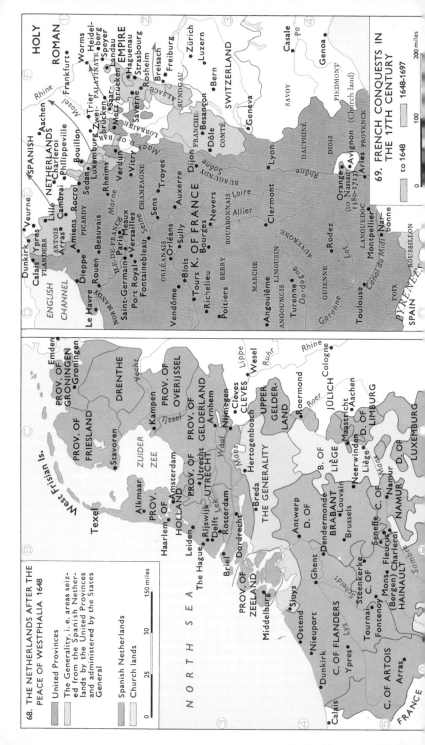

68. THE NETHERLANDS AFTER THE PEACE OF WESTPHALIA 1648

United Provinces

The Generality, i.e. areas seized from the Spanish Netherlands by the United Provinces and administered by the States General

Spanish Netherlands

Church lands

0 25 50   150 miles

NORTH SEA

West Frisian Is.

Texel

Emden
Groningen
PROV. OF GRONINGEN
DRENTHE
PROV. OF FRIESLAND
Stavoren
ZUIDER ZEE
Kampen
Vecht
PROV. OF OVERIJSSEL
IJssel
Alkmaar
PROV. OF HOLLAND
Amsterdam
Haarlem
Utrecht
PROV. UTRECHT
Arnhem
PROV. OF GELDERLAND
Nijmegen
Cleves
CLEVES
Wesel
Lippe
Rhine
Ruhr
Cologne
Leiden
The Hague
Rijswijk
Delft
Lek
Rotterdam
Waal
Maas
Hertogenbosch
Roermond
UPPER GELDERLAND
Jülich
JÜLICH
Roer
Aachen
Briel
Dordrecht
PROV. OF ZEELAND
Breda
THE GENERALITY
B. OF LIÈGE
Maastricht
D. OF LIMBURG
LIMBURG
Middelburg
Sluys
Antwerp
D. OF BRABANT
Louvain
Brussels
Dendermonde
Liège
C. OF LIÈGE
Ostend
Nieuport
Ghent
Scheldt
Seneffe
C. OF NAMUR
Namur
D. OF LUXEMBURG
LUXEMBURG
Dunkirk
C. OF FLANDERS
Ypres
Lys
Tournai
C. OF Steenkerke
Fontenoy
Mons (Bergen)
Charleroi
Fleurus
HAINAULT
Sambre
Calais
C. OF ARTOIS
Arras
FRANCE

69. FRENCH CONQUESTS IN THE 17TH CENTURY

0   100   200 miles

to 1648   1648-1697

HOLY ROMAN EMPIRE

Rhine
Frankfurt
Worms
Heidelberg
Speyer
Landau
Aachen
Trier
Mosel
Luxemburg
Zweibrücken
Saarbrücken
Haguenau
Rosheim
Strasbourg
PALATINATE
Saverne
ALSACE
Breisach
Freiburg
SUNDGAU
Zürich
Luzern
SWITZERLAND
Bern
Geneva
SAVOY
Casale
Po
Genoa
PIEDMONT

SPANISH NETHERLANDS
Veurne
Dunkirk
Ypres
Lille
FLANDERS
Charleroi
Philippeville
Bouillon
ARTOIS
Arras
Cambrai
Rocroi
Sedan
Verdun
Metz
Saar-brücken
MAAS OF BAR
LORRAINE
BAR
Vitry
Rheims
Marne
Meaux
Versailles
Port Royal
Saint-Germain
Fontainebleau
PICARDY
Amiens
Beauvais
ÎLE-DE-FRANCE
Paris
Seine
CHAMPAGNE
Troyes
Sens
Auxerre
Dijon
FRANCHE COMTÉ
Besançon
Dôle
ENGLISH CHANNEL
Dieppe
Rouen
NORMANDY
Le Havre
Calais
Vendôme
Orléans
ORLÉANAIS
Blois
Tours
Richelieu
Poitiers
BERRY
Bourges
Sully
Nevers
BOURBONNAIS
Allier
Loire
Vierzon
BURGUNDY
Saône
Lyon
DAUPHINÉ
DIOIS
Rhône
Orange (to Nassau 1580-1713)
Avignon (Church land)
Arles
PROVENCE
K. OF FRANCE
Angoulême
ANGOUMOIS
LIMOUSIN
MARCHE
Turenne
Dordogne
GUIENNE
Lot
Rodez
AUVERGNE
Clermont
Montpellier
LANGUEDOC
Narbonne
Canal du Midi
Garonne
Toulouse
FOIX
ROUSSILLON
PYRENEES
SPAIN

70. NORTHEASTERN EUROPE IN 1660: EXPANSION OF SWEDEN IN 17TH CENT.

Sweden at the death of Gustavus Vasa, 1560
Conquests 1561-1660
Conquered from Denmark-Norway 1645-60
Duchy of Holstein-Gottorp

Dates show the year of conquest

• Fortresses   Sw. Swedish

0   100   200   300 miles

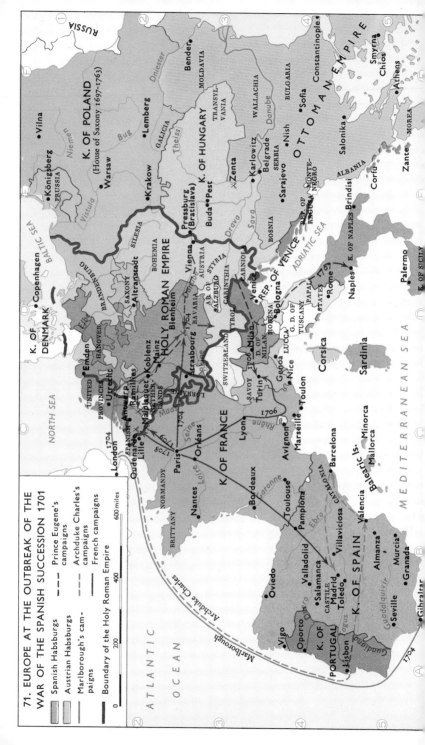

71. EUROPE AT THE OUTBREAK OF THE WAR OF THE SPANISH SUCCESSION 1701

Prince Eugene's campaigns

Archduke Charles's campaigns

Marlborough's campaigns

French campaigns

Boundary of the Holy Roman Empire

Spanish Habsburgs

Austrian Habsburgs

0   200   400   600 miles

72. THE EXPANSION OF RUSSIA FROM 1300 TO 1825

Principality of Moscow *c.* 1300

Grand Duchy of Moscow 1462

Conquests of the Rurik dynasty 1462-1605. Areas subsequently lost are outlined

Expansion between 1643 and 1676

Expansion under Peter the Great 1682-1725

Expansion under Empress Anna 1730-40. Areas subsequently lost are outlined

Expansion under Empress Elizabeth 1741-62

Expansion under Catherine the Great 1762-96

Expansion up to death of Alexander I 1825

0   200   400 miles

ARCTIC OCEAN

NORTH CAPE

NORWAY

LAPLAND

SWEDEN

FINLAND

WHITE SEA

GULF OF BOTHNIA

Archangel

Onega

L. Onega

Nystad

Åbo

Viborg

KARELIA

L. Ladoga

Åland Is.

Kronstadt

Schlüsselburg (Nöteborg)

Visby

Dagö

Narva

St Petersburg

ESTONIA

INGRIA

L. Peipus

Novgorod

Ösel

LIVONIA

NOVGOROD

KOURLAND

Riga

Dvina

Uglitch

KHANATE OF

Viatka

Danzig

PRUSSIA

Volga

Moscow

Oka

Nizhni-Novgorod

Kazan

Kama

Thorn

Vilna

Holovzin

Smolensk

Tula

KAZAN

LITHUANIA

Minsk

Andrussov

Warsaw

POLAND

Pripet

Lesna

Polish 1611-67

Ural

Krakow

MARSHES

Kiev

Volga

GALICIA

UKRAINE (LITTLE RUSSIA)

Kharkov

Don

HUNGARY

Prut

Dniester

Bug

Dnieper

Poltava

Perevolotchna

KHANATE OF

MOLDAVIA

Jassy

Azov

ASTRAKHAN

Astrakhan

TRANSYLVANIA

Bender

KHANATE OF THE CRIMEA

SEA OF AZOV

Kuban

CASPIAN SEA

WALLACHIA

CRIMEA

Terek

Danube

Sevastopol

Kaffa (Feodosiya)

Sofia

Varna

BLACK SEA

CAUCASUS

Adrianople

Batum

Tiflis

Kura

Constantinople

Ardakhan

Kars

Baku

OTTOMAN EMPIRE

Aras

Euphrates

Tigris

PERSIA

73. CAMPAIGN OF CHARLES XII 1700-09

- ▨ Swedish territory at outbreak of Northern War 1700
- │ Charles's campaign. The vertical strokes indicate the beginning of a year
- ‒ ‒ ‒ Charles's journey to Stralsund

0   200   400 miles

74. LITHUANIA AND POLAND 13TH-14TH CENTURIES

- Lithuania 1263
- Expansion 1316-41
- Lithuania at the time of union with Poland 1386
- Expansion of Lithuania 1392-1430
- Poland 1340
- Poland at the time of union with Lithuania 1386

0   200   400 miles

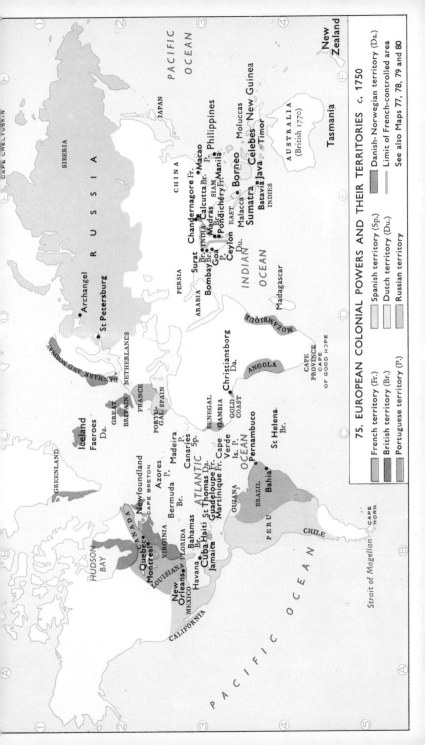

75. EUROPEAN COLONIAL POWERS AND THEIR TERRITORIES c. 1750

French territory (Fr.)

British territory (Br.)

Portuguese territory (P.)

Spanish territory (Sp.)

Dutch territory (Du.)

Russian territory

Danish-Norwegian territory (Da.)

Limit of French-controlled area

See also Maps 77, 78, 79 and 80

Austrian territory
British territory including Hanover, united under the same king 1714-1837
Brandenburg territory
Swedish territory
—— Boundary of Holy Roman Empire

0   200   400 miles

Shetland Is.
Bergen
Orkney Is.
Stavanger
Hebrides
NORTH SEA
Culloden
SCOTLAND Aberdeen
Scone
Falkirk
Glasgow Edinburgh
Berwick
Belfast Newcastle
K. OF GREAT BRITAIN
IRELAND Ripon
Dublin York
Limerick
Newark
Cork Wexford Derby
ENGLAND Southwold
Cambridge
Worcester Oxford London
UNITED
Amsterdam
The Hague Utrecht
PROVINCES Münster
Exeter Chatham
Dover Ostend Colo
Plymouth Portland Dunkirk
AUSTRIAN Aache
Fontenoy
NETHER
CAP DE LA Cambrai LANDS
HOGUE
Rouen Rheims
Brest Versailles Paris Nancy LOR
Rast
Fontainebleau Cirey
Nantes Orléans RAINE S
Seine Loire
Tours Basel
K. OF FRANCE
SWIT
Rochefort Ferney
Limoges Geney
Bordeaux Lyon SAVOY
Garonne Turin
Oviedo Bayonne
Toulouse Avignon
Pamplona Montpellier Marseille
Burgos Toulon
Oporto Valladolid
Ebro
K. OF PORTUGAL
Zaragoza
Duero
Barcelona
Madrid
Tagus Toledo
Lisbon Minorca
(British 1703-83)
Valencia Balearic Is.
Almanza Mallorca
Guadiana
Guadalquivir
Seville
Granada Cartagena MEDITERRANE
Cadiz
Gibraltar
(British 1713)
BARBARY STATES

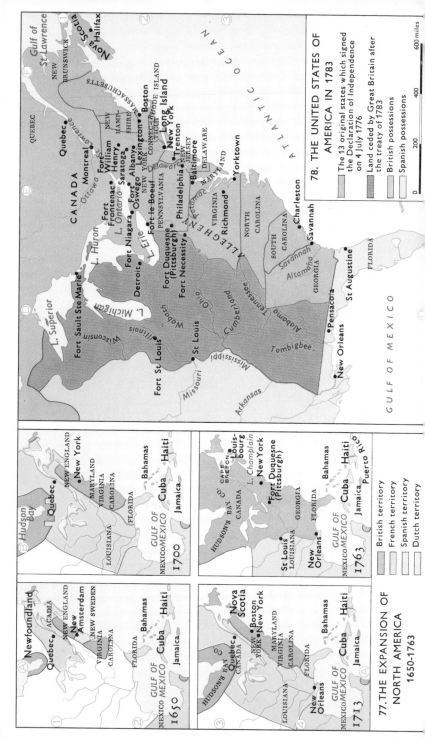

78. THE UNITED STATES OF AMERICA IN 1783

The 13 original states which signed the Declaration of Independence on 4 July 1776

Land ceded by Great Britain after the treaty of 1783

British possessions

Spanish possessions

0   200   400   600 miles

Map 78 labels:

Gulf of St Lawrence · NEW BRUNSWICK · NOVA SCOTIA · Halifax · QUEBEC · Quebec · CANADA · Montreal · Ottawa · L. Superior · Fort Sault Ste Marie · L. Huron · L. Michigan · Wisconsin · Illinois · Fort St Louis · Missouri · Mississippi · Arkansas · St Louis · Fort Frontenac · Fort William Henry · Fort Niagara · L. Ontario · Oswego · Albany · Saratoga · Fort-le-Boeuf · L. Erie · Detroit · Fort Duquesne (Pittsburgh) · Fort Necessity · Ohio · Wabash · Cumberland · Tennessee · ALLEGHENY · PENNSYLVANIA · Philadelphia · NEW YORK · NEW HAMP-SHIRE · MASSACHUSETTS · Boston · RHODE ISLAND · CONNECTICUT · Long Island · New York · NEW JERSEY · Trenton · DELAWARE · Delaware · Baltimore · Potomac · MARYLAND · VIRGINIA · Richmond · Yorktown · NORTH CAROLINA · SOUTH CAROLINA · Charleston · Savannah · GEORGIA · Altamaha · Alabama · Tombigbee · Pensacola · New Orleans · St Augustine · FLORIDA · ATLANTIC OCEAN · GULF OF MEXICO

77. THE EXPANSION OF NORTH AMERICA 1650–1763

1650 (A):
Newfoundland · Quebec · ACADIA · NEW ENGLAND · New Amsterdam · New York · NEW SWEDEN · MARYLAND · VIRGINIA · CAROLINA · FLORIDA · Bahamas · Cuba · Haiti · Jamaica · GULF OF MEXICO

1700 (B):
Hudson Bay · Quebec · NEW ENGLAND · New York · MARYLAND · VIRGINIA · CAROLINA · LOUISIANA · FLORIDA · Bahamas · Cuba · Haiti · Jamaica · GULF OF MEXICO

1713 (C):
HUDSON'S BAY CO · Quebec · CANADA · Nova Scotia · New York · Boston · NEW YORK · MARYLAND · VIRGINIA · CAROLINA · LOUISIANA · New Orleans · FLORIDA · Bahamas · Cuba · Haiti · Jamaica · GULF OF MEXICO

1763 (D):
HUDSON'S BAY CO · CAPE BRETON I. · Louisbourg · CANADA · L. Champlain · New York · Fort Duquesne (Pittsburgh) · GEORGIA · St Louis · LOUISIANA · New Orleans · FLORIDA · Bahamas · Cuba · Haiti · Jamaica · Puerto Rico · GULF OF MEXICO

British territory
French territory
Spanish territory
Dutch territory

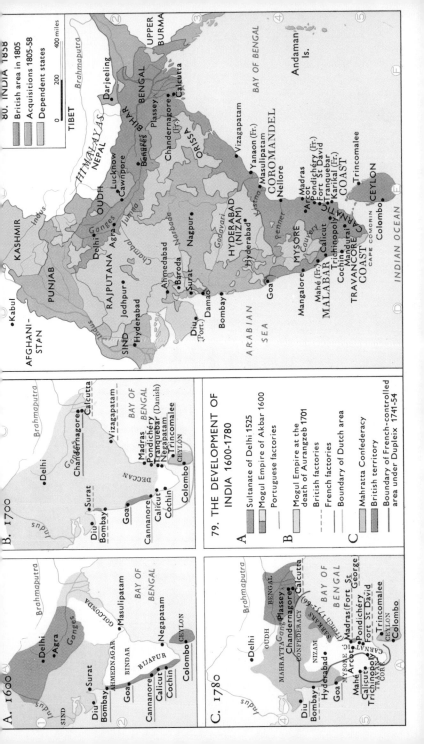

80. INDIA 1858

- British area in 1805
- Acquisitions 1805-58
- Dependent states

0   200   400 miles

Kabul

AFGHANI-STAN

KASHMIR

PUNJAB

Indus

SIND

Hyderabad

Jodhpur

RAJPUTANA

Delhi

Agra

Jumna

Chambal

Ahmedabad

Baroda

Surat

Bombay

Diu (Port.)

Damao

ARABIAN SEA

Goa

HIMALAYAS

TIBET

NEPAL

Darjeeling

Brahmaputra

Ganges

Lucknow

Cawnpore

OUDH

Benares

BIHAR

BENGAL

Plassey

Chandernagore (Fr.)

Calcutta

ORISSA

UPPER BURMA

Nagpur

Narbada

Godavari

HYDERABAD (NIZAM)

Hyderabad

Kistna

Vizagapatam

Yanaon (Fr.)

Masulipatam

COROMANDEL

Nellore

BAY OF BENGAL

Andaman Is.

MYSORE

Cauvery

Penner

Arcot

Madras

Pondichéry (Fr.)

Fort St David

Tranquebar

Karikal (Fr.)

COAST

Mangalore

Mahé (Fr.)

MALABAR

Calicut

Trichinopoly

CARNATIC

Mandura

Trincomalee

Cochin

TRAVANCORE COAST

CAPE COMORIN

Colombo

CEYLON

INDIAN OCEAN

B. 1700

Brahmaputra

Ganges

Delhi

Chandernagore

Calcutta

Vizagapatam

BAY OF BENGAL

BENGAL

Indus

Surat

Diu

Bombay

DECCAN

Goa

Cannanore

Calicut

Cochin

Madras

Pondichéry

Tranquebar (Danish)

Negapatam

Trincomalee

CEYLON

Colombo

---

79. THE DEVELOPMENT OF INDIA 1600-1780

A
- Sultanate of Delhi 1525
- Mogul Empire of Akbar 1600
- Portuguese factories

B
- Mogul Empire at the death of Aurangzeb 1701
- British factories
- French factories
- Boundary of Dutch area

C
- Mahratta Confederacy
- British territory
- Boundary of French-controlled area under Dupleix 1741-54

A. 1600

Brahmaputra

Delhi

Agra

Ganges

GOLCONDA

Masulipatam

BAY OF BENGAL

BENGAL

Indus

SIND

Surat

Diu

Bombay

AHMEDNAGAR

BIDAR

BIJAPUR

Goa

Cannanore

Calicut

Cochin

Negapatam

CEYLON

Colombo

C. 1780

Brahmaputra

Delhi

OUDH

Ganges

Chandernagore

Plassey

Calcutta

BENGAL

MAHRATTA CONFEDERACY

NIZAM

Hyderabad

(SIRKARS (1766))

Indus

Diu

Bombay

Goa

MYSORE

Mahé

Calicut

Trichinopoly

TRAVANCORE

Arcot

Madras (Fort George)

Pondichéry

Fort St David

CARNATIC

Trincomalee

CEYLON

Colombo

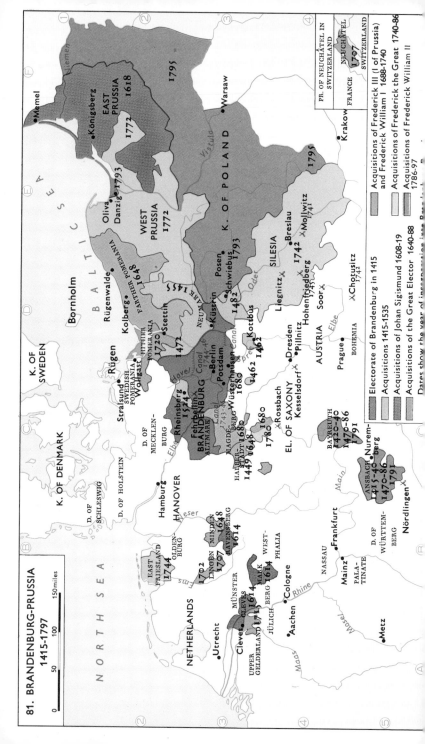

81. BRANDENBURG-PRUSSIA
1415-1797

0 50 100 150 miles

Legend:

- Electorate of Brandenburg in 1415
- Acquisitions 1415-1535
- Acquisitions of Johan Sigismund 1608-19
- Acquisitions of the Great Elector 1640-88
- Acquisitions of Frederick III (I of Prussia) and Frederick William I 1688-1740
- Acquisitions of Frederick the Great 1740-86
- Acquisitions of Frederick William II 1786-97

Dates show the year of incorporation into Prussia

PR. OF NEUCHÂTEL IN SWITZERLAND

PR. OF NEUCHÂTEL IN SWITZERLAND	
FRANCE	NEUCHÂTEL 1707
KRAKOW	SWITZERLAND

Place names and labels:

NORTH SEA

BALTIC SEA

K. OF SWEDEN

K. OF DENMARK

Memel

Königsberg

EAST PRUSSIA 1618

1772

1795

Warsaw

Bornholm

Rügen

Stralsund

SWEDISH POMERANIA

Rügenwalde

Kolberg

FARTHER POMERANIA 1648

HITHER POMERANIA 1720

Stettin

1472

Oliva 1793

Danzig 1793

WEST PRUSSIA 1772

K. OF POLAND

Vistula

Posen 1793

Silesia

Breslau

Mollwitz 1741

1742

Schwiebus 1482

Küstrin

NEUMARK 1455

Liegnitz

Hohenfriedberg 1745

Soor 1745

Chotusitz 1742

D. OF MECKLENBURG

Havel

Berlin

Potsdam

Wüstermark 1680

BRANDENBURG ALTMARK

Rheinsberg 1524

Fehrbellin 1680

Canal 1744-46

1462

Kottbus 1462

Oder

AUSTRIA

BOHEMIA

Prague

Elbe

Dresden

EL. OF SAXONY

Pillnitz

Kesselsdorf 1745

Rossbach

MAGDE-BURG 1680

HALBER-STADT 1648 1449

1780

Hamburg

HANOVER

Weser

Elbe

Ems

EAST FRIESLAND 1744

OLDENBURG

LINGEN 1702

MINDEN 1648

RAVENSBERG 1614

1707

BAYREUTH 1420-40 1791

Nuremberg

ANSBACH 1415-40 1470-86 1791

Nördlingen

MÜNSTER

CLEVES

MARK 1614

BERG

JÜLICH

WEST-PHALIA

UPPER GELDERLAND 1713

NETHERLANDS

Utrecht

Aachen

Cologne

Rhine

NASSAU

Frankfurt

Mainz

PALA-TINATE

D. OF WÜRTTEM-BERG

Maas

Mosel

Metz

D. OF SCHLESWIG

D. OF HOLSTEIN

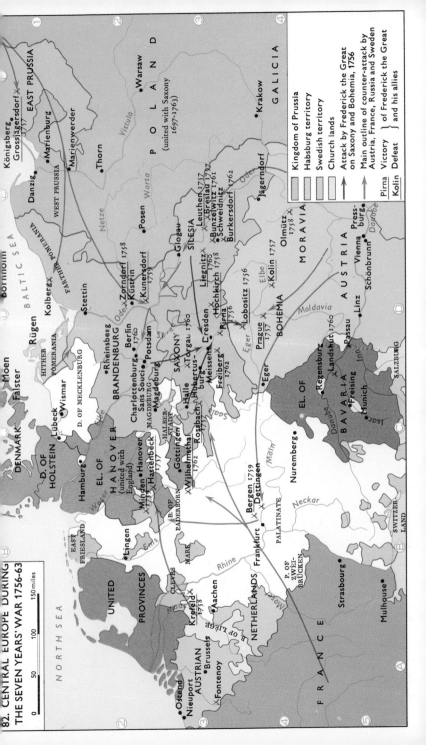

82. CENTRAL EUROPE DURING THE SEVEN YEARS' WAR 1756-63

0   50   100   150 miles

Legend:

- Kingdom of Prussia
- Habsburg territory
- Swedish territory
- Church lands
- → Attack by Frederick the Great on Saxony and Bohemia, 1756
- → Main outline of counter-attack by Austria, France, Russia and Sweden
- Pirna — Victory } of Frederick the Great and his allies
- Kolin — Defeat }

NORTH SEA
BALTIC SEA

Moen
Falster
Bornholm
Rügen
Kolberg ×
HITHER POMERANIA
FARTHER POMERANIA
Königsberg ×
Grossjägersdorf × 1757
EAST PRUSSIA
Marienburg
Danzig
WEST PRUSSIA
Marienwerder
Thorn
Warsaw

DENMARK
D. OF HOLSTEIN
Lübeck
Wismar
Hamburg ×
D. OF MECKLENBURG

Stettin
Küstrin × Zorndorf 1758
Kunersdorf 1759
BRANDENBURG
Rheinsberg
Berlin
Charlottenburg · Sans Souci · Potsdam
MAGDEBURG
Magdeburg

Posen
Warta
Netze
Vistula
P O L A N D
(united with Saxony 1697-1761)

Glogau
SILESIA
Leuthen 1757 ×
Breslau 1757 ×
× Bunzelwitz 1761
Liegnitz 1760 ×
Schweidnitz 1758 ×
Burkersdorf 1762

EL. OF HANOVER
(united with England)
Hanover ×
Minden × 1759
Hastenbeck × 1757
Göttingen ×
Wilhelmstal 1762
B. OF PADERBORN
HALBER-STADT
Halle
Rossbach × 1757
Saale

Dresden ×
Pirna × 1756
Meissen ×
Torgau 1760 ×
Hubertus-burg
Freiberg × 1762
SAXONY

Hochkirch × 1758
Lobositz 1756 ×
Eger
Elbe
Prague × 1757
Kolin 1757 ×
B O H E M I A
Moldavia

Olmütz × 1758
Jägerndorf
Oder
M O R A V I A
Pressburg
Vienna
Schönbrunn
Danube

EAST FRIESLAND
Lingen
UNITED PROVINCES
CLEVES
MARK
Krefeld × 1758
Aachen
B. OF LIÈGE
Brussels
AUSTRIAN NETHERLANDS
Ostend
Nieuport ×
Fontenoy ×

EL. OF BAVARIA
Regensburg
Landshut 1760 ×
Freising
Munich
Isar
SALZBURG
A U S T R I A
Linz
Passau
Inn

Wilhelmstal
Bergen 1759 ×
Dettingen ×
Frankfurt
PALATINATE
P. OF ZWEI-BRÜCKEN
Nuremberg
Neckar
Main
Rhine
Mosel
SWITZER-LAND
Strasbourg
Mulhouse

F R A N C E

GALICIA

Wesel
Ems
Weser
Eger
Saale
Moldavia
Danube

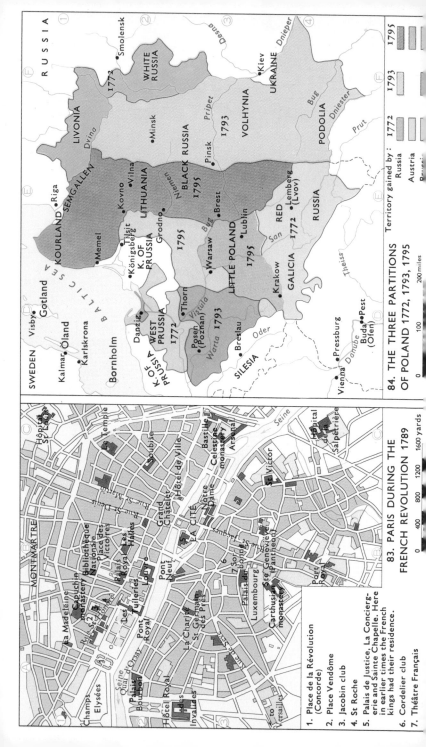

84. THE THREE PARTITIONS OF POLAND 1772, 1793, 1795

Territory gained by: 1772   1793   1795
Russia
Austria
Prussia

0   100   200 miles

RUSSIA

SWEDEN
Gotland
Visby
Öland
Kalmar
Karlskrona
Bornholm

BALTIC SEA

Riga
Memel
LIVONIA
KOURLAND
SEMGALLEN
1772
WHITE RUSSIA
Smolensk
Desna
Dnieper
Kiev
UKRAINE
Minsk
Pripet
1793
VOLHYNIA
Bug
Dniester
PODOLIA
Prut
RED RUSSIA
Lemberg (Lvov)
1772
GALICIA
Krakow
San
Theiss
Danube
Pressburg
Vienna
SILESIA
Breslau
Oder
Warta
Posen (Poznan)
1793
Thorn
WEST PRUSSIA
1772
Vistula
Danzig
K. OF PRUSSIA
Königsberg
Tilsit
Grodno
1795
LITHUANIA
Niemen
Vilna
Kovno
BLACK RUSSIA
1795
Pinsk
Brest
Bug
Lublin
LITTLE POLAND
1795
Warsaw
Buda (Ofen)
Pest
Dvina
RUSSIA

83. PARIS DURING THE FRENCH REVOLUTION 1789

0   400   800   1200   1600 yards

MONTMARTRE
La Madeleine
Capuchin monastery
Bibliothèque Nationale
Place des Victoires
Rue St-Denis
Le Temple
Soubise
Hôpital St-Louis
Bastille
Celestine monastery
Arsenal
Hôtel de Ville
Grand Châtelet
Notre Dame
LA CITÉ
Seine
Palais Royal
Tuileries
Pont Neuf
Pont Royal
Quai d'Orsay
Champs Elysées
Palais Bourbon
Hôtel Royal des Invalides
to Versailles
Palais du Luxembourg
Ste Geneviève (Pantheon)
La Charité
St Germain des Prés
Carthusian monastery
St Victor
Hôpital de la Salpêtrière

1. Place de la Révolution (Concorde)
2. Place Vendôme
3. Jacobin club
4. St Roche
5. Palais de Justice, La Conciergerie and Sainte Chapelle. Here in earlier times the French kings had their residence.
6. Cordelier club
7. Théâtre Français

85. ITALY c. 1800

French territory:

- France 1792
- Piedmont, seized from Sardinia 1798
- Duchy of Parma, seized 1803

States under French control:

- Cisalpine Republic 1797-1802, Italian Republic 1802-05
- Ligurian Republic 1797-1805
- Papal States, Roman Republic 1797-1805
- Republic of Lucca 1799-1805
- K. of Naples (Parthenopean Republic) 1799
- K. of Etruria 1801-08
- Pr. of Piombino 1801
- K. of Italy 1805
- K. of Sardinia before 1798
- Rep. of Venice, Austrian 1797-1805

0   100   200 miles

86. EUROPE IN NAPOLEON'S TIME 1812

ATLANTIC OCEAN

SCOTLAND

Glasgow • Edinburgh

Belfast •

NORTH SEA

K. OF GREAT BRITAIN

IRELAND • Dublin

• Manchester
• Liverpool

ENGLAND

• Birmingham

• Bristol

Old Sarum • • London

Plymouth • Dover

Southampton • Boulogne • Calais

ENGLISH CHANNEL

Eu • Waterloo

• Brest

Rouen • • Amiens

Châtillon • Malmaison • Rheims • Paris

Versailles • Saint-Cloud

Fontainebleau • Brienne

Orléans • Chaumont

Nantes

VENDÉE

F R E N C H

E M P I R E

Bordeaux • Lyon • Geneva

Turin •

Cape
Finisterre
✕
(1805)

• Oviedo

• Bayonne

• Vitoria

Oporto (1808)

K. OF

PORTUGAL

Fuentes de Onoro

Torres Vedras

Cintra •

Lisbon •

Talavera • Toledo
(1809)

Madrid (1808)

Zaragoza

ANDORRA

• Barcelona

K. OF SPAIN

• Valencia

Bailen

• Seville

Cadiz • Gibraltar

Cartagena

Balearic Is.
Mallorca

Minorca
(Br. 1798-1802)

M E D I T E R R A

✕ Cape
Trafalgar
(1805)

Ceuta

MOROCCO

• Oran

• Algiers

ALGERIA

• Constantine

• Tunis

TUNIS

Bergen •

Christian

Toveru
Prestebak

• Christian

Götebor

Flads

Hälsing

Copenhag

Kie

K. OF DENMARK AND NORWAY

HOLLAND • Amsterdam

K. OF
WEST-
PHALIA

CON

• Antwerp

Ghent •

Brussels • Gross-Görsch

Aix-la- Auerstädt
Chapelle Erfurt

Ligny • Koblenz K. OF
SAXONY

Varennes Karlsb

Hambach •

Verdun

Lunéville • Ettenheim

Basel • Hohenlinde

Zürich • BAV.

Bern

HELVETIAN
REPUBLIC

FEDERAT
OF T

K. OF
WÜRTTEM- K. (
BERG Muni

BADEN

RHINE

K. OF

• Milan • Verona

Venic

• Parma

Savona • Genoa ITA

Marseille • Nice

Toulon • Cannes

LUCCA • Flo

Elba PIOMBI

Corsica

Ajaccio •

Rome

K. OF

SARDINIA

• Cagliari

Pale

TRIPC

Legend

French territory

States ruled by Members of
Napoleon's family

Other French-controlled areas

Allies of France

Great Britain and British
territory

Neutral states

— — — Napoleon's Eastern campaign 1798

———— Wellington's Spanish camp. 1808-9

———— Napoleon's Russian campaign 1812

0   200   400 miles

FINLAND
Viborg
L. LADOGA
Åbo
Helsingfors
St Petersburg
Sveaborg
Åland
Reval
Novgorod
ESTONIA
Stockholm
Volga
EDEN Gotland
LIVONIA
Öland
Riga
Borodino
Moscow
Iskrona
KOURLAND
Dvina
Vitebsk
olm
Tilsit
Smolensk
Königsberg
Vilna
RUSSIAN
REP. OF
Friedland
DANZIG
Eylau
OF PRUSSIA
Niemen
Berezina
n
EMPIRE
G. D. OF
Pripet
Posen
Warsaw
Vistula
Trachenberg
Kiev
utzen
WARSAW
Oder
sden
Dnieper
rague
Münchengrätz
HEMIA
Krakow
rünn
Troppau
GALICIA
Brno
MORAVIA
Dniester
sterlitz
AUSTRIAN
Wagram
BESSARABIA
enna
Aspern
Essling
MOLDAVIA
Odessa
nbrunn
Pressburg
CRIMEA
Buda
Pest
SLOVENIA
EMPIRE
TRANSYLVANIA
BLACK SEA
Agram
aibach
SLAVONIA
BANAT
WALLACHIA
RIAN PROVINCES
BOSNIA
Belgrade
Bucharest
SERBIA
Danube
MONTE-
BULGARIA
NEGRO
Sofia
OF
Adrianople
RUMELIA
ECORVO
BENEVENTO
Constantinople
aples
OTTOMAN
Salerno
Salonika
NAPLES
Corfu
Lemnos
(French)
EMPIRE
Ionian Is.
1797 Fr.
Chios
1799 Russ, 1809 Br.
MOREA
Athens
OF
ICILY
Navarino
Rhodes
Cyprus
Malta
Crete
SYRIA
Acre
SEA
Jaffa
Aboukir
Alexandria
Cairo
EGYPT

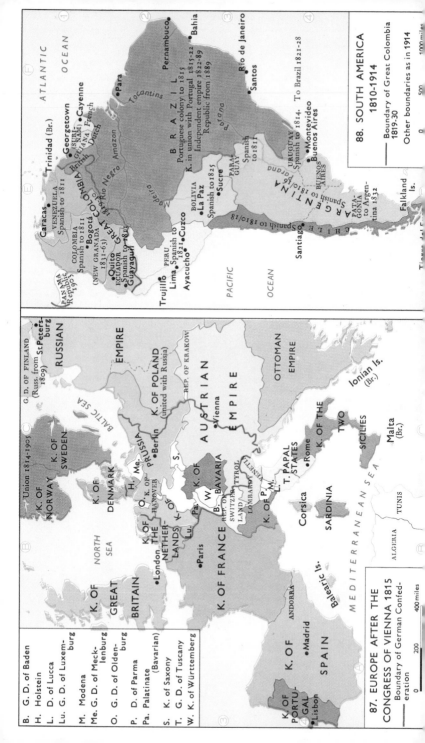

87. EUROPE AFTER THE CONGRESS OF VIENNA 1815

▬▬▬ Boundary of German Confederation

B. G. D. of Baden
H. Holstein
L. D. of Lucca
Lu. G. D. of Luxemburg
M. Modena
Me. G. D. of Mecklenburg
O. G. D. of Oldenburg
P. D. of Parma
Pa. Palatinate (Bavarian)
S. K. of Saxony
T. G. D. of Tuscany
W. K. of Württemberg

0   200   400 miles

G. D. OF FINLAND (Russ. from 1809)
RUSSIAN EMPIRE
St. Petersburg
Union 1814-1905
K. OF NORWAY
K. OF SWEDEN
BALTIC SEA
K. OF POLAND (united with Russia)
REP. OF KRAKOW
K. OF DENMARK
NORTH SEA
GREAT BRITAIN
K. OF HANOVER
PRUSSIA
Berlin
AUSTRIAN EMPIRE
Vienna
K. OF THE NETHERLANDS
London
Paris
K. OF FRANCE
SWITZERLAND
TYROL
K. OF BAVARIA
LOMBARDY
VENETIA
REP. OF
PAPAL STATES
Rome
K. OF THE TWO SICILIES
SARDINIA
Corsica
K. OF PORTUGAL
Lisbon
K. OF SPAIN
Madrid
ANDORRA
Balearic Is.
MEDITERRANEAN SEA
ALGERIA
TUNIS
Malta (Br.)
Ionian Is. (Br.)
OTTOMAN EMPIRE

88. SOUTH AMERICA 1810-1914

▬▬▬ Boundary of Great Colombia 1819-30
Other boundaries as in 1914

0   500   1000 miles

ATLANTIC OCEAN
Trinidad (Br.)
Caracas
VENEZUELA Spanish to 1811
Georgetown British Guiana
SURINAM Dutch
Cayenne French Guiana
GREAT COLOMBIA
COLOMBIA Spanish to 1819
(NEW GRANADA 1831-63)
Bogotá
Para
Amazon
Rio Negro
Madeira
ECUADOR Spanish to 1822
Quito
Guayaquil
PERU Spanish to 1821
Trujillo
Lima Spanish to 1826
Ayacucho
Cuzco
BOLIVIA Spanish to 1825
La Paz
Sucre
B R A Z I L
Portuguese colony to 1815
K. in union with Portugal 1815-22
Independent empire 1822-89
Republic from 1889
Pernambuco
Bahia
Tocantins
Rio de Janeiro
Santos
To Brazil 1821-28
PARAGUAY Spanish to 1811
URUGUAY Spanish to 1814. To Brazil 1821-28
Montevideo
Buenos Aires
ARGENTINA Spanish to 1810/16
CHILE Spanish to 1810/18
Santiago
PATAGONIA to Argentina 1832
Falkland Is.
PACIFIC OCEAN
PANAMA Republic 1903

89.-90. UNIFICATION OF ITALY 1859-70

89. NORTHERN ITALY 1859

Dates show the year of incorporation into the Kingdom of Sardinia

0   25   50 miles

SWITZERLAND

Rhône
Adige

TYROL

A U S T R I A

Adda
Lake Maggiore
Lake Como

LOMBARDY
1859

Piave

VENETIA

•Trieste

ISTRIA

K. OF
Novara•
×Magenta
•Milan

PIEDMONT

Ticino

Solferino•
•Lodi

Solferino ×

Lake Garda
×Verona
Custozza
×Villafranca
•Mantua

Padua•
Venice•

Po

•Pavia
•Cremona

•Piacenza

Adige
Po

•Adria

•Alessandria

D. OF PARMA
1860

Guastalla
(to Parma)
D. OF
MODENA
1860

•Ferrara

ROMAGNA
1860

SARDINIA

Parma

90. THE KINGDOM OF SARDINIA

SWITZERLAND

AUSTRIAN EMPIRE

SAVOY
(Fr. 1860)

TYROL

LOMBARDY
•Milan
Solferino•

VENETIA
1866
•Venice

•Trieste

CROATIA

K. OF

•Turin
PIEDMONT

Po

SARDINIA
Genoa•

FRENCH

D. OF
PARMA

D. OF
MODENA

ROMAGNA

TURKEY

5 May 1860

NICE
(Fr. 1860)

•Florence

PAPAL

•Zara
DALMATIA

EMPIRE
•MONACO
Nice

G. D. OF
TUSCANY

STATES

A
D
R
I
A
T
I
C

S
E
A

Elba

UMBRIA

Corsica

1870

•Rome

Caprera

Sardinia

Garibaldi

PONTECORVO
Gaëta•
•Capua

BENEVENTO

Naples• 7 Sept. 1860 K. OF

•Salerno

THE

T Y R R H E N I A N

S E A

TWO

Palermo Messina•
• 26 Aug. 1860
Reggio•

Marsala•
11 May 1860

Sicily

SICILIES

M E D I T E R R A N E A N   S E A

Sardinia 1859

Austria and Austrian territory 1859

Sardinia, Spring 1860

To Kingdom of Sardinia, Autumn 1860

Garibaldi's exp. against the Two Sicilies

Dates are given for the incorporation of Venetia and the remaining Papal States into the K. of Italy

0   100   200   300 miles

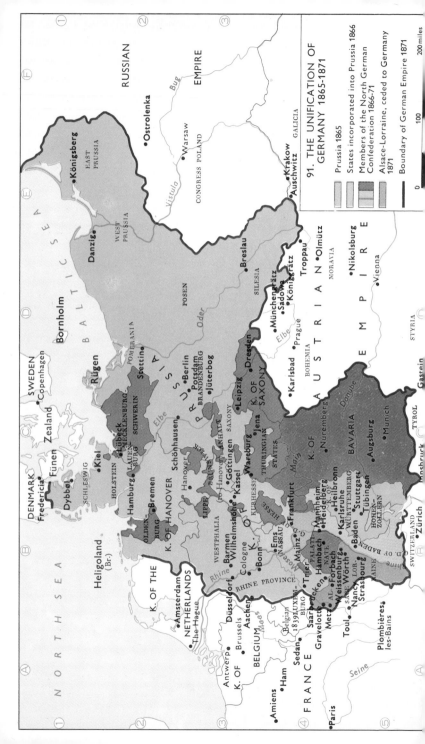

91. THE UNIFICATION OF GERMANY 1865-1871

Prussia 1865

States incorporated into Prussia 1866

Members of the North German Confederation 1866-71

Alsace-Lorraine, ceded to Germany 1871

Boundary of German Empire 1871

0   100   200 miles

RUSSIAN EMPIRE

NORTH SEA

BALTIC SEA

SWEDEN

Copenhagen

DENMARK
Fredericia
Dybbøl
Zealand
Funen

Bornholm

Heligoland (Br.)

Königsberg
EAST PRUSSIA

Danzig
WEST PRUSSIA

Rügen
POMERANIA

Kiel
SCHLESWIG
HOLSTEIN

Lübeck
LAUEN-BURG
MECKLENBURG-SCHWERIN

Hamburg
Bremen
OLDEN-BURG

Stettin
Oder

Berlin
Potsdam
BRANDENBURG
Jüterbog

Ostrolenka
Bug

Warsaw
CONGRESS POLAND

Vistula

POSEN

Breslau
SILESIA

Krakow
Auschwitz
GALICIA

Troppau
Olmütz
MORAVIA
Nikolsburg

Vienna

K. OF THE NETHERLANDS
Amsterdam
The Hague

K. OF HANOVER
Schönhausen
Hanover
(to Hanover)
Göttingen
ANHALT
SAXONY

Schwerin
Elbe

Leipzig
Dresden
K. OF SAXONY
THURINGIAN STATES
Jena
Warburg

Karlsbad
BOHEMIA
Prague
Elbe

Münchengrätz
Sadowa
Königgrätz

AUSTRIAN EMPIRE

STYRIA

WESTPHALIA
Barmen
LIPPE
Wilhelmshöhe
KURHESSE
Kassel

Düsseldorf
Cologne
Bonn
RHINE PROVINCE
Aachen

BELGIUM
K. OF
Antwerp
Brussels
Belgian
Maas
1839 LUXEMBURG

Ham
Amiens
Paris
Seine

FRANCE
Sedan
Gravelotte
Mons
Trier
LUXEMBURG
Saarbrücken
AL. LOR.
Metz
SAXE
Nancy
Toul
Wörth
Wörth
Strasbourg

Plombières-les-Bains

Frankfurt
NASSAU
Ems
Mainz
HESSE
Main
PALATINATE
Mannheim
Heidelberg
NAT.
Hambach
Forbach
Weisenburg
Karlsruhe
Heilbronn
Stuttgart
BADEN
WÜRTTEMBERG
Tübingen
HOHEN-ZOLLERN

Nuremberg
K. OF BAVARIA
Augsburg
Munich

Rhine
SWITZERLAND
Zürich
Rhine
TYROL
Innsbruck

Gastein

Danube

92. THE UNITED STATES OF AMERICA 1783-1912 * THE CIVIL WAR 1861-65

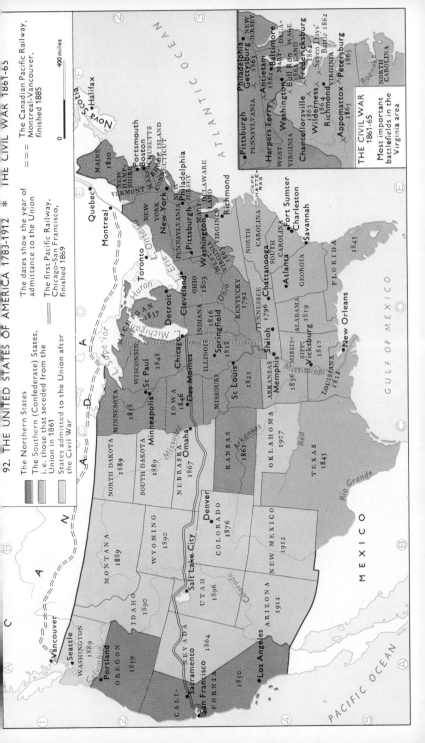

The Northern States

The Southern (Confederate) States, i.e. those that seceded from the Union in 1861

States admitted to the Union after the Civil War

The dates show the year of admittance to the Union

=== The Canadian Pacific Railway, Montreal–Vancouver, finished 1885

─── The first Pacific Railway, Chicago–San Francisco, finished 1869

THE CIVIL WAR 1861-65

Most important battlefields in the Virginia area

Philadelphia • NEW JERSEY
Gettysburg 1863
PENNSYLVANIA
Pittsburgh •
Harpers Ferry × Antietam
Baltimore
WEST VIRGINIA
Washington ×× Bull Run MARY-LAND DELA-WARE
Chancellorsville ×× Fredericksburg 1862
Wilderness × 1863 × Seven Days' Battle 1862
Richmond •× 1864 VIRGINIA
Appomattox ×× Petersburg 1865
Roanoke
NORTH CAROLINA

Map labels

ATLANTIC OCEAN
PACIFIC OCEAN
GULF OF MEXICO
MEXICO
CANADA

Vancouver
Seattle
WASHINGTON 1889
Portland
OREGON 1859
Sacramento
San Francisco
CALIFORNIA 1850
Los Angeles
NEVADA 1864
IDAHO 1890
MONTANA 1889
WYOMING 1890
UTAH 1896
Salt Lake City
COLORADO 1876
Denver
ARIZONA 1912
NEW MEXICO 1912
NORTH DAKOTA 1889
SOUTH DAKOTA 1889
NEBRASKA 1867
Omaha
KANSAS 1861
OKLAHOMA 1907
TEXAS 1845
MINNESOTA 1858
Minneapolis
St. Paul
IOWA 1846
Des Moines
MISSOURI 1821
St. Louis
ARKANSAS 1836
LOUISIANA 1812
New Orleans
WISCONSIN 1848
ILLINOIS 1818
Chicago
Springfield
MICHIGAN 1837
INDIANA 1816
OHIO 1803
KENTUCKY 1792
TENNESSEE 1796
MISSISSIPPI 1817
ALABAMA 1819
GEORGIA
Atlanta
FLORIDA 1845
Detroit
Cleveland
Memphis
Vicksburg
Shiloh
Chattanooga
NORTH CAROLINA
SOUTH CAROLINA
Charleston
Savannah
Fort Sumter
Richmond
VIRGINIA
WEST VIRGINIA
PENNSYLVANIA
Pittsburgh
Washington
Philadelphia
NEW YORK
New York
New Jersey
DELAWARE
MARYLAND
CONNECTICUT
RHODE ISLAND
MASSACHUSETTS
Boston
NEW HAMPSHIRE 1820
VERMONT
MAINE
Portsmouth
Quebec
Montreal
Toronto
Halifax
Nova Scotia
NEWFOUND-LAND
PRINCE EDWARD ISLAND

Rivers and lakes
Columbia
Colorado
Rio Grande
Red
Arkansas
Missouri
Mississippi
Ohio
L. Superior
L. Michigan
L. Huron
L. Erie
L. Ontario
CAPE HATTE-RAS

0   400 miles

93. THE BALKANS AFTER THE CONGRESS OF BERLIN 1878

Turkish territory, occupied and administered by Austria-Hungary

Boundary of the large Bulgaria proposed by Russia in the preliminary treaty of San Stefano

0   100   200   300 miles

RUSSIA

Dniester
BESSARABIA
Prut
MOLDAVIA
• Jassy

CRIMEA
Eupatoria •
Sevastopol • • Alma
• Inkerman
Balaklava

Romanian 1856-78

AUSTRIA-HUNGARY
WALLACHIA
• Bucharest
• Belgrade
BOSNIA
SERBIA
ROMANIA
Danube
DOBRUJA

BLACK SEA
• Sinope

HERZEGO-VINA
DALMATIA
• Sarajevo
MONTE-NEGRO
Plevna •
BULGARIA
(under Turkish suzerainty)
• Sofia
EAST RUMELIA
Shipka Pass

ADRIATIC SEA

ALBANIA

Adrianople • • Constantinople
San Stefano • • Scutari
• Ankara

T
U
R

Gallipoli •
Sea of
Marmara
• Brussa

ITALY
Salonika •

DARDANELLES

Ionian Is.
(to Greece 1863)

THESSALY

AEGEAN
SEA

Lesbos
Chios
• Smyrna

GREECE • Athens

MOREA

Navarino •

Rhodes

Cyprus
(Br. 1878)

94. THE BALKANS AFTER THE WARS OF 1912-13

0   100   200   300 miles

RUSSIA

Prut *Dniester*

CRIMEA
• Sevastopol

AUSTRIA-HUNGARY
TRANSYLVANIA
Drava
Theiss
SLAVONIA
BANAT
Sava
ROMANIA
• Bucharest
Danube
DOBRUJA

BLACK SEA

BOSNIA
(Annexed 1908)
• Belgrade
• Sarajevo
HERZEGOVINA
(Annexed 1908)
SERBIA
MONTE-NEGRO

BULGARIA
• Sofia
• Adrianople
• Constantinople
• Ankara

ADRIATIC SEA
ALBANIA
• Durazzo
MACEDONIA
THRACE

T
U
R
K
E
Y

ITALY
• Salonika
Lemnos

AEGEAN
SEA
Lesbos

THESSALY
1881

Corfu
Chios

GREECE • Athens

Dodecanese
(Ital. from 1912)

MOREA
Rhodes

Crete
(Greek 1908/12)

Cyprus

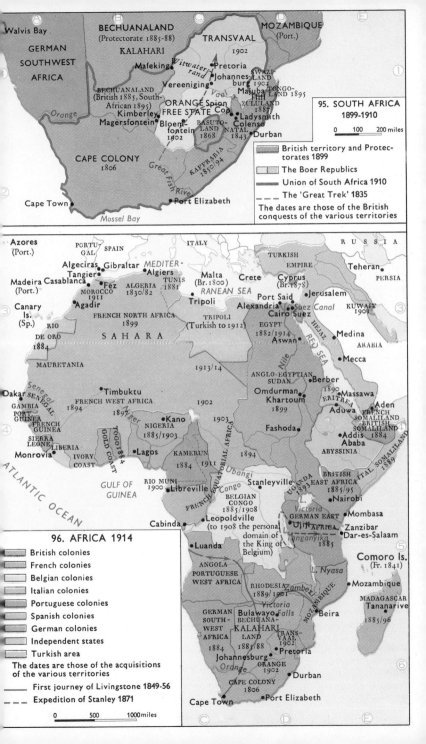

95. SOUTH AFRICA 1899-1910

0   100   200 miles

- British territory and Protectorates 1899
- The Boer Republics
- Union of South Africa 1910
- The 'Great Trek' 1835

The dates are those of the British conquests of the various territories

Walvis Bay
GERMAN SOUTHWEST AFRICA
BECHUANALAND (Protectorate 1885-88)
KALAHARI
TRANSVAAL
MOZAMBIQUE (Port.)
1902
Mafeking
Witwatersrand
Pretoria
Johannesburg
SWAZILAND 1902
BECHUANALAND (British 1885, South-African 1895)
Vereeniging
Vaal
Majuba TONGOLAND 1895
Orange
ORANGE FREE STATE 1899
Spion Cop
Fili
ZULULAND 1887
Kimberley
Magersfontein
Bloemfontein 1902
BASUTOLAND 1868
Ladysmith
Colenso
NATAL 1843
Durban
CAPE COLONY 1806
Great Fish River
KAFFRARIA 1850/52
Cape Town
Port Elizabeth
Mossel Bay

96. AFRICA 1914

- British colonies
- French colonies
- Belgian colonies
- Italian colonies
- Portuguese colonies
- Spanish colonies
- German colonies
- Independent states
- Turkish area

The dates are those of the acquisitions of the various territories

- First journey of Livingstone 1849-56
- Expedition of Stanley 1871

0   500   1000 miles

Azores (Port.)
PORTUGAL
SPAIN
ITALY
TURKISH EMPIRE
RUSSIA
Teheran
PERSIA
Algeciras
Gibraltar
MEDITERRANEAN SEA
Malta (Br. 1800)
Crete
Cyprus (Br. 1878)
Tangier
Algiers
TUNIS 1881
Madeira Casablanca (Port.)
Fez
ALGERIA 1830/82
Tripoli
Port Said
Alexandria
Jerusalem
Canary Is. (Sp.)
MOROCCO 1911
Agadir
Cairo Suez
Suez Canal
KUWAIT 1901
RIO DE ORO 1884
FRENCH NORTH AFRICA
TRIPOLI (Turkish to 1912)
EGYPT 1882/1914
Aswan
HEJAZ
Medina
SAHARA
ARABIA
Mecca
MAURETANIA
1913/14
ANGLO-EGYPTIAN SUDAN
Berber 1890
Massawa
Dakar
Senegal
Timbuktu
FRENCH WEST AFRICA
1902
Omdurman
Khartoum 1899
ERITREA
Aden
GAMBIA
SENEGAL 1894
1897
Niger
1903
Fashoda
Aduwa
FRENCH SOMALILAND 1884
BRITISH SOMALILAND
PORT. GUINEA
FRENCH GUINEA
NIGERIA 1885/1903
Kano
Addis Ababa
ITAL. SOMALILAND 1889
SIERRA LEONE
LIBERIA
TOGO 1884
GOLD COAST
Lagos
KAMERUN 1884
1911
ABYSSINIA
Monrovia
IVORY COAST
1894
Ubangi
GULF OF GUINEA
RIO MUNI 1900
Libreville
FRENCH EQUATORIAL AFRICA
Congo
Stanleyville
UGANDA 1893
BRITISH EAST AFRICA 1885/95
Nairobi
ATLANTIC OCEAN
BELGIAN CONGO 1885/1908
L. Victoria
GERMAN EAST AFRICA
Mombasa
Cabinda
Leopoldville (to 1908 the personal domain of the King of Belgium)
Ujiji
L. Tanganyika 1885
Zanzibar
Dar-es-Salaam
Luanda
ANGOLA PORTUGUESE WEST AFRICA
L. Nyasa
Comoro Is. (Fr. 1841)
Mozambique
RHODESIA 1889/1901
Zambesi
Victoria Falls
MOZAMBIQUE
MADAGASCAR Tananarive 1885/96
Beira
GERMAN SOUTHWEST AFRICA 1884
Bulawayo
BECHUANALAND 1885/88
KALAHARI
TRANSVAAL 1902
Johannesburg
Pretoria
Orange
ORANGE 1902
Durban
CAPE COLONY 1806
Cape Town
Port Elizabeth

Ⓐ Ⓑ Ⓒ

•Simbirsk

•Sverdlovsk •Tobolsk
(Ekaterinburg)

Samara• Trans-Siberian railway. Finished 1904.

①
•Constantinople

TURKEY

Don

Volga

MEDI-
TERRA-
Cyprus   •Kars
NEAN SEA   Baku•

•Astrakhan

ARAL
SEA   L. Balkhash

•Alexandria   CASPIAN SEA
•Cairo   •Beirut
Suez
Canal

②   Russian
Sphere
1907   •Teheran

WEST TURKESTAN
Khiva• 1847/73

TURK-
MENISTAN   Bokhara• •Tashkent
1881/86   Samarkand•
•Merv

BOKHARA

SINKIA

RED SEA

Euphrates
Tigris

KUWAIT
1901

ARABIA

PERSIA

PAMIR
1893

AFGHANISTAN   •Kabul

KASHMIR
1846

•Kandahar   PUNJAB
1890   1849
British   •Lahore •Amritsar
Sphere
1907   BALUCHISTAN
1876

③   •Mecca

PERSIAN GULF

British
Sphere
1893

OMAN
(under British
Protection)   •Muscat

•Karachi

Indus

SIND

Delhi• •Meerut
RAJPUTANA   NEPA
Agra• OUDH   HIMALA
•1856
•Cawnpore •Luckno

BRITISH   Benares•

Ganges

ERITREA

•Aden
FR.
SOMALILAND

HADRAMAUT

ARABIAN SEA

Diu•
(Port.) •Damão
(Port.)   INDIA   Chander
(Fr.

④
BRITISH
SOMALILAND

Socotra

•Bombay

ETHIOPIA

ITAL. SOMALILAND

Goa•
(Port.) Hyderabad•
NIZAM

•Yanaor

MYSORE
Bangalore•   •Madras
Mahé• •Pondichéry (F
(Fr.) •Karikal (Fr.)

⑤

INDIAN

CEYLON
Colombo•

97. ASIA 1914

Russia 1800   Russian sphere of interest
Russian acquisitions 1800-78   British sphere of interest
Russian acquisitions 1878-1914   French sphere of interest
British territory   Japanese sphere of interest
French territory   German sphere of interest
Japanese territory
American territory   The dates are those of the acqui-
Dutch territory   sitions of the various territories.
See also Maps 75 and 80

OCEAN

0   200 400 600 800 1000 miles

Ⓒ

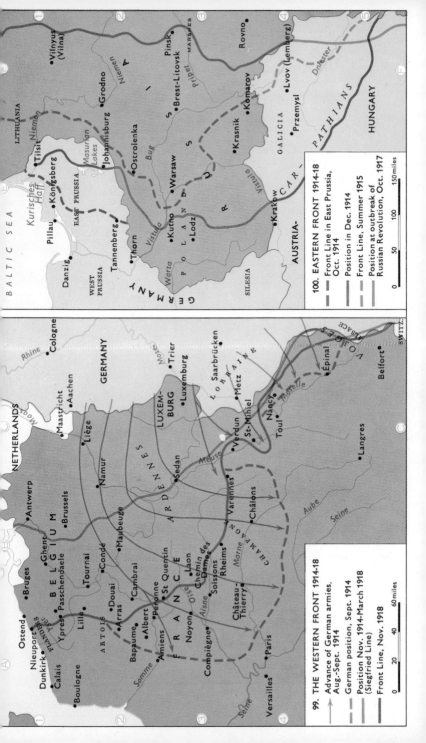

99. THE WESTERN FRONT 1914-18

→ Advance of German armies,
Aug.–Sept. 1914

━━━ German position, Sept. 1914

━ ━ ━ Position Nov. 1914–March 1918
(Siegfried Line)

━━━ Front Line, Nov. 1918

0	20	40	60 miles

100. EASTERN FRONT 1914-18

━ ━ ━ Front Line in East Prussia,
Oct. 1914

━━━ Position in Dec. 1914

━ ━ ━ Front Line, Summer 1915

━━━ Position at outbreak of
Russian Revolution, Oct. 1917

0	50	100	150 miles

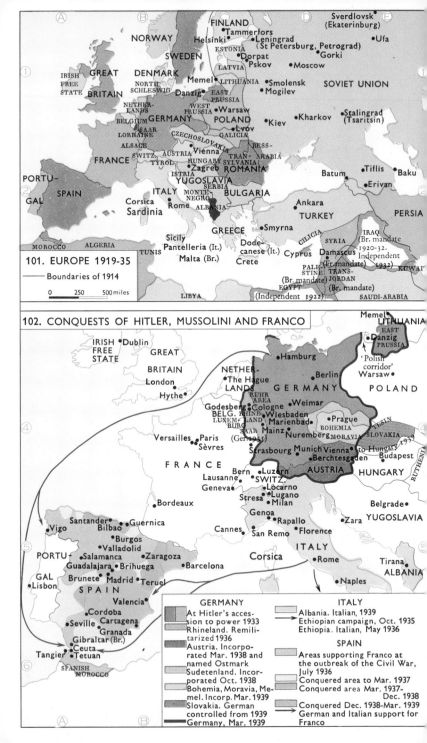

101. EUROPE 1919-35

— Boundaries of 1914

0   250   500 miles

Sverdlovsk (Ekaterinburg)
FINLAND
Tammerfors
NORWAY   Helsinki   •Leningrad
(St Petersburg, Petrograd)   •Ufa
SWEDEN   ESTONIA   •Gorki
Dorpat
DENMARK   LATVIA   Pskov   •Moscow
IRISH   GREAT   Memel   •Smolensk   SOVIET UNION
FREE   BRITAIN   NORTH   Danzig   LITHUANIA   •Mogilev
STATE   SCHLESWIG   EAST
NETHER-   WEST   PRUSSIA
LANDS   PRUSSIA   Warsaw   •Kiev   •Kharkov   •Stalingrad
BELGIUM   GERMANY   POLAND   (Tsaritsin)
SAAR   •Lvov
LORRAINE   CZECHOSLOVAKIA   GALICIA
ALSACE   AUSTRIA   Vienna   BESS-
FRANCE   SWITZ.   TYROL   HUNGARY   ARABIA
ISTRIA   Zagreb   TRAN-
SYLVANIA   ROMANIA   •Tiflis   •Baku
PORTU-   YUGOSLAVIA   •Batum
SPAIN   MONTE-   SERBIA   BULGARIA   •Erivan
GAL   Corsica   NEGRO   Rome   ALBANIA
Sardinia   ITALY   Ankara
•Smyrna   TURKEY   PERSIA
MOROCCO   ALGERIA   GREECE   Dode-   Cyprus
TUNIS   Sicily   canese (It.)   SYRIA   IRAQ (Br. mandate)
Pantelleria (It.)   CILICIA   Damascus   1920-32.
Malta (Br.)   Crete   (Fr.mandate)   Independent
PALE-   TRANS-   1932
STINE   JORDAN   KUWAIT
(Br. mandate)   (Br. mandate)
LIBYA   EGYPT   SAUDI-ARABIA
(Independent 1922)

102. CONQUESTS OF HITLER, MUSSOLINI AND FRANCO

Memel
LITHUANIA
IRISH   •Dublin   EAST
FREE   GREAT   Danzig   PRUSSIA
STATE   BRITAIN   •Hamburg   'Polish
corridor'
NETHER-   •Berlin   Warsaw •
London   •The Hague   GERMANY   POLAND
Hythe•   LANDS   RUHR
AREA
Godesberg•Cologne   •Weimar
BELG.   RHINE-   Wiesbaden   •Prague
LUXEM-   LAND   Marienbad   BOHEMIA   TESIN
Versailles•Paris   BURG   SAAR   Mainz   Nuremberg   MORAVIA   SLOVAKIA
Sèvres•   (Ger.1935)   Strasbourg•Munich Vienna   to Hungary 1939
Berchtesgaden   •Budapest
FRANCE   Bern   •Luzern   AUSTRIA   HUNGARY   RUTHENIA
Lausanne•   SWITZ.
Geneva•   •Locarno
•Lugano   Belgrade•
Bordeaux•   Stresa•   •Milan   YUGOSLAVIA
Genoa   •Rapallo   •Zara
Santander•   •Guernica   Cannes•   San Remo   •Florence
Vigo•   Bilbao•   •Burgos   ITALY
•Valladolid   •Rome   Tirana•
PORTU-   •Salamanca   •Zaragoza   Corsica   ALBANIA
GAL   Guadalajara•   •Brihuega   •Barcelona
•Lisbon   Brunete•Madrid   •Teruel   •Naples
SPAIN
Valencia•
•Cordoba
•Seville   Cartagena•
•Granada
Gibraltar (Br.)
Tangier•   •Tetuan
SPANISH   •Ceuta
MOROCCO

GERMANY	ITALY
At Hitler's accession to power 1933	Albania. Italian, 1939
Rhineland. Remilitarized 1936	Ethiopian campaign, Oct. 1935
Austria. Incorporated Mar. 1938 and named Ostmark	Ethiopia. Italian, May 1936
Sudetenland. Incorporated Oct. 1938	SPAIN
Bohemia, Moravia, Memel. Incorp. Mar. 1939	Areas supporting Franco at the outbreak of the Civil War, July 1936
Slovakia. German controlled from 1939	Conquered area to Mar. 1937
Germany, Mar. 1939	Conquered area Mar. 1937-Dec. 1938
	Conquered Dec. 1938-Mar. 1939
	German and Italian support for Franco

103. EUROPE DURING THE SECOND WORLD WAR, SEPT. 1939-JUNE 1941

Legend:
- Western Powers at outbreak of war 3 Sept. 1939
- Germany, Sept. 1939
- Italy at war with Western Powers, June 1940, and Bulgaria at war with Great Britain, Mar. 1941
- Soviet Union, non-aggression pact with Germany from Aug. 1939-June 1941
- Neutral countries, Sept. 1939
- Axis advances to June 1941
- Russian advances to June 1940
- Russian boundary, June 1940
- Occupied area of France after 26 June 1940

The light red boundaries show the political situation in Sept. 1939. Dates indicate time of German occupation.

0   200   400   600 miles

ICELAND

Petsamo
Murmansk
Narvik
Salla
Suomussalmi
FINLAND War with Russia Nov. 1939
Namsos
Steinkjer
Andalsnes
Trondhjem
NORWAY
Elverum
Mar. 1940
Bergen
Hamar Helsinki
Viborg
Oslo
SWEDEN
Stavanger
Christiansand
Stockholm
Leningrad
ESTONIA June 1940
EIRE
GREAT DENMARK 1940
LATVIA June 1940
Dublin
BRITAIN
Liverpool
LITHUANIA
Coventry
Danzig
Minsk
London
NETHER-LANDS
Berlin
Sept. 1939
Dunkirk
BELGIUM
GERMANY
Warsaw
Kiev
Rouen
LUXEM-BURG
POLAND
Sept. 1939
1940
Paris
Prague
1939
FRANCE
Munich
SLOVAKIA BUKOVINA June 1940
Vichy
Bern
Vienna
Bordeaux
SWITZ.
HUNGARY
BESSARABIA
Toulouse
Milan
ROMANIA
PORTU-GAL
Marseille
Belgrade
Bucharest
Lisbon
Madrid
Corsica
Rome
YUGOSLAVIA
SOUTH DOBRUJA
SPAIN
Sardinia
ITALY
1941
BUL-GARIA
(Bulg. Sept. 1940)
Gibraltar (Br.)
Naples
ALBANIA (It.)
Sofia
Sp.Tangier
T U R K E Y
Ankara
PERSIA
MOROCCO
ALGERIA (Fr.)
TUNISIA (Fr.)
Sicily
GREECE 1941
Athens
SYRIA (Fr. mandate)
IRAQ
(Fr.)
Malta
Crete
Cyprus (Br.)

104. EUROPE DURING THE SECOND WORLD WAR, OCT. 1942-MAY 1945

0   400   800 miles

Legend:
- Germany and its allies 1942
- Area under German and Ital. control Oct. 1942
- Area under Allied control Oct. 1942
- Neutral countries 1942

FINLAND armistice 4 Sept. 1944
Viborg June 1944
SWEDEN
Helsinki
Leningrad
Stockholm
GREAT
Edinburgh
Riga
Moscow
DENMARK
EIRE
Copenhagen
Vilnyus
Katyn
SOVIET
BRITAIN
Hamburg
Lübeck
Danzig
Minsk
Smolensk
Voronesh
London
NETHER-LANDS
Bergen-Belsen
Warsaw
Brest-Litovsk
UNION
Arnhem
Berlin
Torgau
Contentin
Caen BELGIUM
Cologne
Remagen
POLAND
Stalingrad
BRITTANY
Schweinfurt
Buchenwald
Auschwitz
Kiev
Kharkov
Falaise
Paris
Prague
Lvov
Argentan
Aug. 1944
Pilsen
SLOVAKIA
Dachau
Nuremberg
Stalino
Munich
Vienna
Vichy
Berchtes-gaden
Budapest
Crimea
Bordeaux
Lyon
SWITZ.
HUNGARY
Yalta
Milan
CAUCASUS
ROMANIA
Madrid
Belgrade
SPAIN
Corsica
YUGOSLAVIA
BULGARIA
Istanbul
Rome
ITALY
Sofia
Ankara
PORTUGAL
Sardinia
Sept. 1943
Naples
ALBANIA
T U R K E Y
British troops
Amer. and Brit. troops Nov. 1942
Oran
Algiers
Tunis May 1943
Sicily July 1943
GREECE
Cyprus
MOROCCO
ALGERIA
British troops
Malta
Crete
SYRIA
IRAQ
PALE-STINE
Tripoli Jan. 1943
Tobruk Nov. 1942
El Alamein
Alexandria
JORDAN
LIBYA
Benghazi Nov. 1942
EGYPT
ARABIA

Front lines May 1944
Front lines Dec. 1944
Allied advances
Black boundaries show the political situation in September 1939

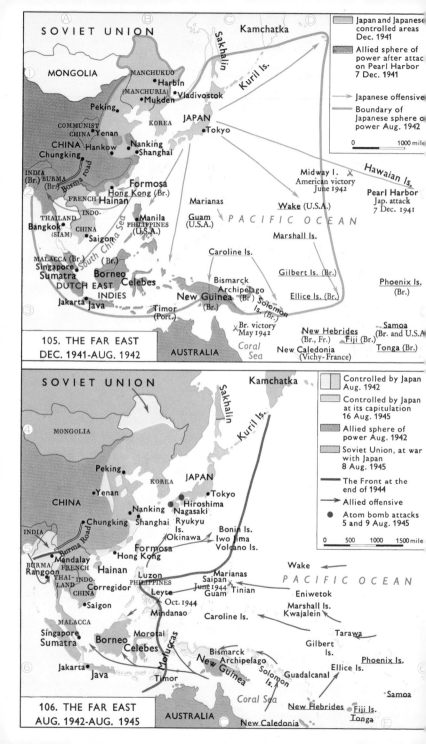

Map 105. THE FAR EAST DEC. 1941–AUG. 1942

Legend:
- Japan and Japanese controlled areas Dec. 1941
- Allied sphere of power after attack on Pearl Harbor 7 Dec. 1941
- Japanese offensive
- Boundary of Japanese sphere of power Aug. 1942

0 — 1000 miles

SOVIET UNION
MONGOLIA
MANCHUKUO (MANCHURIA) • Harbin
• Mukden • Vladivostok
Peking •
COMMUNIST CHINA • Yenan
KOREA
CHINA
Hankow • Nanking
Chungking • • Shanghai
JAPAN • Tokyo
INDIA (Br.) BURMA (Br.)
Burma road
Formosa
FRENCH INDO-CHINA
Hong Kong (Br.)
Hainan
THAILAND (SIAM)
Bangkok •
Saigon •
Manila PHILIPPINES (U.S.A.)
MALACCA (Br.)
Singapore (Br.)
Sumatra
Borneo
Celebes
DUTCH EAST INDIES
Jakarta • Java
Timor (Port.)
South China Sea
Marianas
Guam (U.S.A.)
Midway I. American victory June 1942
Wake (U.S.A.)
Hawaian Is.
Pearl Harbor Jap. attack 7 Dec. 1941
PACIFIC OCEAN
Marshall Is.
Caroline Is.
Gilbert Is. (Br.)
Phoenix Is. (Br.)
Bismarck Archipelago (Br.)
New Guinea (Br.)
Solomon Is. (Br.)
Ellice Is. (Br.)
Br. victory May 1942
New Hebrides (Br., Fr.)
Fiji (Br.)
Samoa (Br. and U.S.A.)
Tonga (Br.)
New Caledonia (Vichy-France)
Coral Sea
AUSTRALIA

105. THE FAR EAST DEC. 1941–AUG. 1942

Map 106. THE FAR EAST AUG. 1942–AUG. 1945

Legend:
- Controlled by Japan Aug. 1942
- Controlled by Japan at its capitulation 16 Aug. 1945
- Allied sphere of power Aug. 1942
- Soviet Union, at war with Japan 8 Aug. 1945
- The Front at the end of 1944
- Allied offensive
- Atom bomb attacks 5 and 9 Aug. 1945

0 — 500 — 1000 — 1500 mile

SOVIET UNION
Kamchatka
Sakhalin
Kuril Is.
MONGOLIA
CHINA
Peking •
• Yenan
KOREA
JAPAN
• Tokyo
Nanking • Hiroshima
Chungking • Shanghai Nagasaki
Burma Road
Ryukyu Is.
Okinawa
Bonin Is.
Iwo Jima
Volcano Is.
INDIA
BURMA
Mandalay •
Rangoon •
FRENCH THAI-INDO-LAND CHINA
Formosa
Hong Kong
Hainan
Saigon •
Luzon PHILIPPINES
Corregidor
Leyte Oct. 1944
Mindanao
Wake
Marianas
Saipan June 1944
Guam Tinian
PACIFIC OCEAN
Eniwetok
Marshall Is. Kwajalein
Caroline Is.
MALACCA
Singapore •
Sumatra
Borneo
Morotai
Celebes
Moluccas
Timor
Jakarta • Java
Tarawa
Gilbert Is.
Phoenix Is.
Bismarck Archipelago
New Guinea
Solomon Is.
Guadalcanal
Ellice Is.
Samoa
Coral Sea
New Hebrides
Fiji Is.
Tonga
AUSTRALIA
New Caledonia

106. THE FAR EAST AUG. 1942–AUG. 1945

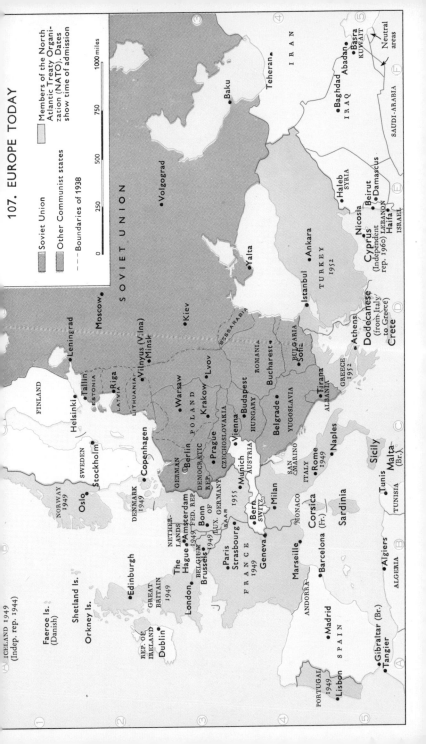

107. EUROPE TODAY

Members of the North Atlantic Treaty Organization (NATO). Dates show time of admission

Soviet Union

Other Communist states

--- Boundaries of 1938

0 250 500 750 1000 miles

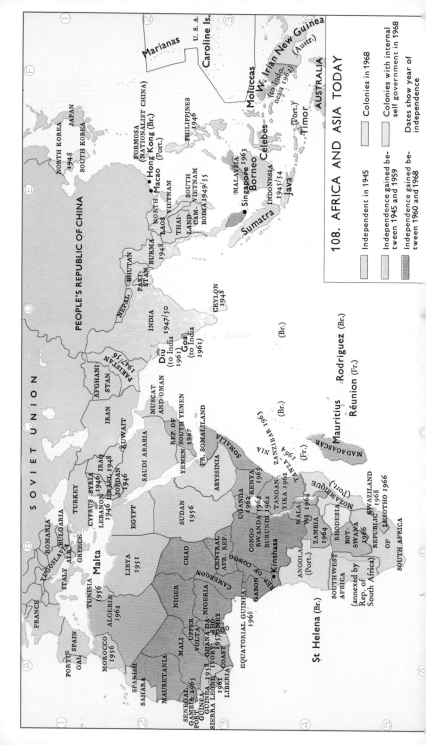

108. AFRICA AND ASIA TODAY

■ Independent in 1945

Colonies in 1968

▨ Independence gained between 1945 and 1959

Colonies with internal self government in 1968

▨ Independence gained between 1960 and 1968

Dates show year of independence

SOVIET UNION

FRANCE
PORTUGAL
SPAIN
ITALY
YUGOSLAVIA
ROMANIA
BULGARIA
ALBANIA
GREECE
TURKEY
CYPRUS
SYRIA
LEBANON 1946
ISRAEL 1948
JORDAN 1946
IRAQ 1946
KUWAIT
SAUDI ARABIA
IRAN
AFGHANISTAN
PAKISTAN 1947/56

PEOPLE'S REPUBLIC OF CHINA

NEPAL
BHUTAN
INDIA 1947/50
Diu (to India 1961)
Goa (to India 1961)
CEYLON 1948

JAPAN
NORTH KOREA 1948
SOUTH KOREA
FORMOSA (NATIONALIST CHINA)
Hong Kong (Br.)
Macao (Port.)
BURMA 1948
THAILAND
LAOS
NORTH VIETNAM
SOUTH VIETNAM
CAMBODIA 1949/55
PHILIPPINES 1946

Marianas
U.S.A.
Caroline Is.

MALAYSIA 1963
Singapore 1963
Sumatra
Borneo
Celebes
INDONESIA 1945/54
Java
Timor (Port.)
Moluccas
W. Irian New Guinea (to Indonesia 1963)
New Guinea (Austr.)
AUSTRALIA

MOROCCO 1956
TUNISIA 1956
ALGERIA 1962
SPANISH SAHARA
MAURETANIA
MALI
NIGER
LIBYA 1951
EGYPT
SUDAN 1956
CHAD
SENEGAL
GAMBIA 1965
PORTUGUESE GUINEA
GUINEA 1958
SIERRA LEONE 1961
LIBERIA
IVORY COAST 1960
GHANA 1957
UPPER VOLTA
TOGO 1960
DAHOMEY 1960
NIGERIA
CAMEROON
CENTRAL AFR. REP.
EQUATORIAL GUINEA 1968
GABON
REP. OF CONGO
Kinshasa
REP. OF CONGO
UGANDA 1962
KENYA 1963
RWANDA 1962
BURUNDI 1962
CONGO 1960
ABYSSINIA
FR. SOMALILAND
SOMALIA
REP. OF YEMEN/SOUTH YEMEN 1967
MUSCAT AND OMAN

TANGANYIKA 1962
ZANZIBAR 1963
TANZANIA 1964
MALAWI 1964
ZAMBIA 1964
ANGOLA (Port.)
RHODESIA
BOTSWANA 1966
REPUBLIC OF SOUTH AFRICA
SOUTH AFRICA
SOUTHWEST AFRICA (annexed by Rep. of South Africa)
LESOTHO 1966
SWAZILAND 1968
MOZAMBIQUE (Port.)

St Helena (Br.)

MADAGASCAR
Mauritius
Rodriguez (Br.)
Réunion (Fr.)

INDEX

The index contains all the place names on the maps, and also names of peoples (e.g. Goths), historical events (e.g. Civil War in England), military expeditions (e.g. Marlborough), voyages of discovery (e.g. Columbus), etc.

Towns and cities which appear on more than one map are generally given a reference to only one map—the one on which they are most important historically, or, for very common names, the one on which they can be most easily found, i.e. generally the map drawn to the largest scale.

More than one reference is given to places important at different times for different reasons. Poitiers, for example, has a reference to Map 33—the battle between Charles Martel and the Moslems in 732—and to Map 43, where it is shown as important in the civilization of medieval Europe.

Countries, provinces, regions, etc.—the boundaries of which may alter with time—are given several references in chronological order, so that their development may be traced. Bulgaria, for example, has sixteen references for the period 900 to 1968; and if one is interested in the political situation in Italy at the beginning of the eighteenth century there are references to two maps, showing the situation in 1701 and 1721.

For references to wide historical periods or concepts which cannot be immediately found in the index, the list of contents at the beginning of the book should be consulted.

The italic number is the number of the map; the letter and number which follow show the area on the map in which the name will be found. (It is to be supposed that each map is divided into squares by lines drawn down the page midway between the letters and across the page midway between the numbers.)

Names in parentheses are alternative names or spellings; those preceded by *mod.* are the modern or present-day names of the localities. Classical names of towns and cities are given in their Latin form.

Aachen (Aix-la-Chapelle)
 *36*C4, *43*C2, *61*D4, *67*B3
Aalborg *44*C2, *70*A4
Aargau *48*C5
Aarhus *70*A4
Abadan *107*F5
Abdera (*mod.* Adra), Spain *11*A3
Abdera, Thrace *14*D1
Aberdeen *65*D2
Åbo *72*A3
Aboukir *86*F6
Abruzzi *45*E4
Abu Simbel *2*A4
Abusir *2*A1
Abydos, Egypt *1*B3, *2*A3
Abydus, on the Hellespont *14*E1
Abyla *11*A3
Abyssinia (Ethiopia)
 1914 *96*E4, 1968 *108*C3
Acadia *77*A1
Acarnania *14*A2
Acco (Acre) *41*B5
Achaea, ancient *14*B3
 during Persian Wars *20*B3
 Roman province *28*D4, *29*C4
 1230 *40*D4   1265 *52*A2
 1355 *53*A5
Achaeans *12*
Achelous (river) *14*B2
Acqui *49*D5
Acrae *16*C3
Acragas (Agrigentum,
 mod. Agrigento) *16*B3
Acre *40*F5, *41*B5, *86*F6
Acropolis, Athens *13*, *17*
Actium *14*A2, *28*D3
Adab *8*C4
Adalia *60*C4
Adana *41*B1
Adda (river) *89*B1
Addis Ababa *96*E4
Aden, 1914 *97*A4
Adige (river) *89*C1–2
Adria *89*D2
Adrianople (*mod.* Edirne)
 *32*E4, *40*E3, *52*B1
Aduatuca *27*F1
Aduwa *96*E4
Aegates Is. *23*C3
Aegean Sea *20*C–D1–5
Aegina (island, *mod.* Aigina) *15*C6
Aegina (town, *mod.* Aigina) *15*C6
Aegira *15*A6
Aegitium *15*A5
Aegium *15*A5
Aegospotami *21*F2
Aegyptus
 44 B.C. *28*E5   A.D. 117 *29*D5
 See also Egypt
Aemilius Paulus, trophy of,
 Delphi *19*C4
Aenus (*mod.* Enez) *11*E2
Aeolians *14*
Aequi *23*C2
Aetolia *14*B2

Afghanistan, 814 *33*F2
 1914 *97*B–C3   1968 *108*C2
Africa (Roman province)
 146 B.C. *25*C5   44 B.C. *28*C4
 A.D. 117 *29*B4
Africa (continent)
 c. 1600 *58*C–D3–5
 1750 *75*C–D3–4
 1914 *96*   1968 *108*
Agadir *96*A3
Agedincum (*mod.* Sens) *27*E2
Agen *49*B5
Agincourt *51*C3
Agra *80*E2
Agram *86*D4
Agrigentum
 (Acragas, *mod.* Agrigento) *16*B3
Ahmedabad *80*D3
Ahmednagar *79*A2
Aigues-Mortes *40*A2
Aire *49*B5
Aisne (river) *99*B3
Aix(-en-Provence) *43*C4, *49*C5
Aix-la-Chapelle (Aachen) *86*C3
 See also Aachen
Ajaccio *85*A3
Akbar *see* Mogul Empire
Akershus (county), 1660 *70*A–B3
Akershus *70*B3
Akhetaton
 (*mod.* Tell-el-Amarna) *2*A2
Akkad *8*B–C4
Alabama (river) *78*D4
Alabama (state), 1861–65 *92*D4
Alaça Hüyük *6*B1
Alais *49*C5
Alalakh (*mod.* Tell Atchana) *6*C2
Alamannia *36*C5
Alamans, 526 *32*C3
Åland Is.
 1370 *44*D1   1660 *70*C3
 1812 *86*D1   1825 *72*A3
Alaric, route of *32*E4
Alba, central Italy *21*A1
Alba, north Italy *49*C5
Albania
 1265 *52*A2   1556 *57*D4
 1701 *71*E4–5 1721 *76*E5
 1812 *86*D4–5 1878 *93*B2
 1912–13 *94*B5–6
 1914–18 *98*D4 1919–35 *101*C2
 1939 *102*E5   1939–41 *103*C3
 1945 *104*C5–6 1968 *107*C4–5
Albano *39*D5
Albany *78*E2
Albenga *49*D5
Albert *99*A2
Albi *43*B4, *51*C6
Albret *50*A6
Alcibiades' journey to Sicily,
 415 B.C. *21*
Alençon *61*C3
Aleppo *41*D2
Aleria *25*E2
Alesia *27*E2

Ansbach
    1415–40, 1470–86, 1791 *81*C5
    1648 *67*C4
Antietam *92*F4
Anti-Lebanon *9*F1
Antilles, Greater *56*C-E1
Antioch, Syria *see* Antiochia
Antioch, Principality of
    1140 *41*C2–3   1265 *52*E2
Antiochia, Persia *20*F3
Antiochia (Antioch, *mod.* Antakya)
    Syria *29*D4, *41*C2
Antoninus and Faustina, Temple of
    Rome *31*C6(5)
Antwerp *43*C2, *44*A5, *61*C3
Anyang *1*E2
Aosta *49*C4
Apaches *59*B3
Apamea *26*B3
Apennines *25*E2
Aphroditopolis *2*A2
Apollo, Sanctuary of, Delphi *19*
Apollo Sitalkas, Delphi *19*B4
Apollonia *11*E2
Appenzell *48*D5
Appomattox *92*E5
Aptara *12*B
Apulia, 264 B.C. *23*D2
    10th century *38*D5
    1100 *39*D5
Aqua Appia, Rome *30*D-E3
Aquae Sextiae
    (*mod.* Aix-en-Provence) *27*F4
Aquileia (*mod.* Aglar) *32*C3
Aquincum (*mod.* Budapest) *29*C2
Aquino *45*E4
Aquitaine, 1100 *39*B-C4
    1180–1453 *50*   1429 *51*B5
Aquitania, *c.* 50 B.C. *27*D-E4
    A.D. 117 *29*A-B2
    843 *36*B5
    See also Aquitaine
Arabia (Roman province) *29*D5
Arabia
    632–814 *33*   1914 *97*A2–4
    1914–18 *98*E-F5
Arabian Sea *97*B4
Arachosia *7*E6
Aragon, 1037 *54*E1
    c. 1100 *54*B2, *39*B5
    1180 *54*E2   1230 *40*A3
    1476 *55*D-E4–5
Aral Sea *10*E1
Aranjuez *55*C5
Ararat, Mt. *6*D1
Aras (river) *72*D-E6
Arausio (*mod.* Orange) *27*F4
Araxes (river) *10*C2
Arbe *49*E5
Arbela (*mod.* Erbil) *22*C3
Arcadia *14*B3, *15*A6
Arcadians *14*
Archangel *72*C2
Arcole *85*B1
Arcot *79*A5, *80*E4
Arctic Ocean *58*F1

Ardakhan *72*D6
Ardennes *99*B-C2
Arelate (*mod.* Arles) *27*F4
Arendal *70*A3
Arezzo *45*D3
Argentan *104*B5
Argentina, 1914 *88*E3–5
Argentoratum
    (*mod.* Strasbourg) *29*B2
Argolis *14*C3, *15*B6
Argos (state) *20*B4
Argos (town) *21*D3
Aria *22*E3
Ariminum (*mod.* Rimini) *23*C1
Arizona, 1912 *92*A-B4
Arkansas (river) *59*B3-C4, *92*C4
Arkansas (state), 1861–65 *92*C-D4
Arles *39*C4
Armagh *43*A1
Armagnac, 1429 *51*B-C6
Armenia, 600 B.C. *7*B-C5
    44 B.C. *28*F2–3
    A.D. 117 *29*E3
    814 *33*D2   1230 *40*F4
    1520–1680 *60*E3
Arnhem *44*B4, *61*D3, *104*B4
Arno (river) *45*C-D3
Arques *62*C2
Arras *49*B2, *51*D3, *99*A2
Arretium (*mod.* Arezzo) *23*B1
Artaxata *29*E3
Artemis of Brauron, Temple of
    Acropolis, Athens *17*B4
Artemisium, Greece *20*C3
Artemisium, Spain *11*B3
Artois, 1429 *51*D3
    1579 *61*A4   1914–18 *99*A2
Arx, Rome *31*A5
Ascalon
    1400 B.C. *6*B3   860 B.C. *9*D4
    A.D. 1140 *41*A6
Asclepius, Temple of
    Acropolis, Athens *17*C-D5
Ascoli *45*E3
Asculum *23*C2
Ashur *8*B2
Asia (Roman province) *28*E3, *29*D3
Asia (continent)
    c. 1300 *42*, 1914 *97*, 1968 *108*
Asia Minor, 189 B.C. *26*
Asine *15*B6
Asisium (*mod.* Assisi) *29*B3
Asklepios (Asclepius), Temple of
    Acropolis, Athens *17*C-D5
Askra *15*B5
Aspern *86*D3
Assam, 1914 *97*D4
Assassins *41*C3
Assen *67*E1
Assiniboine (river) *59*C3
Assisi *43*D4, *45*D3
Assiut *2*A2
Assyria
    1400 B.C. *6*D2
    greatest expansion of Empire
    c. 700 B.C. *7*A-C5–6

B

Brabant
   1429 *51*E3
   1579 *61*C-D3–4
Bradford *65*D3
Braga *55*A5
Brahestad *70*D2
Brahmaputra (river) *80*F2
Brandenburg (town) *44*C4
Brandenburg-Prussia
   1415–1797 *81*   *c.* 1630 *64*D4
   1648 *67*C-D2   1700 *73*B2
   1701 *71*D1–2   1721 *76*D3
Bratislava (Pressburg) *71*E3
Brazil
   c. 1600 *58*B4   1750 *75*B-C4
   1815–1914 *88*E-F1–4
Breda *61*C3
Breida Fjord *37*A1
Breisach *69*F2
Breisgau, 1648 *67*B5
Breitenfeld *64*D5
Bremen *38*B1, *43*C1, *44*B4, *67*C2
Bremen, Archbishopric of
   c. 1630 *64*C4
   1648 *67*C2
Brenner Pass *38*C3
Brescia *45*C1
Breslau *44*D5, *82*E3
Brest-Litovsk *100*F3
Brétigny *51*C4
Bretland (Wales) *37*B2
Briel *61*C3
Brienne *86*C3
Brihuega *102*B5
Brindisi *38*E5
Bristol *65*D4
Britannia *28*B1
Britannia Inferior, A.D. 117 *29*B1
Britannia Minor (Brittany) *32*B2
Britannia Superior, A.D. 117 *29*A1
British colonies, 1750 *75*
British East Africa, 1914 *96*E4–5
British Guiana (*mod.* Guyana)
   1914 *88*E1
British India, 1914 *97*B-D3–5
   See also India
British (Celtic) kingdoms
   526 *32*A-B1–2
British Somaliland
   1914 *96*E4, *97*A4
Brittany (Britannia Minor) *32*B2
   814 *33*A3   843 *36*A4
   c. 900 *37*B3   1100 *39*B3
   1180–1453 *50*   ·1429 *51*A4
Brixen *49*D4
Brixen, Bishopric of, 1648 *67*C6
Brno (Brünn) *86*D3
Bromley, London *66*E6
Brompton, London *66*A6
Brömsebro *70*B4
Bruges *44*A5, *61*B3
Brule, route of *59*C3
Brundisium (*mod.* Brindisi) *23*E2
Brunete *102*A5
Brünn (Brno) *86*D3

Brunswick *44*C4
Brunswick, Duchy of, 1871 *91*C3
Brussa *60*C3
Brussels *43*C2, *61*C4
Bruttium *23*D3
Bucephala *22*F3
Bucharest *60*C2, *76*F4, *93*C1
Buchenwald *104*C5
Buckingham *65*D4
Buckingham Palace, London *66*B6
Buda *39*E4, *43*D3, *60*B1
Budapest *98*C4, *104*C5, *107*C4
Buenaventura *56*D2
Buenos Aires (province) *88*E4
Buenos Aires (town) *88*E4
Bug (river running into Black Sea)
   *74*C-D6
Bug (tributary of the Vistula)
   *74*B5
Bulawayo *96*D6
Bulgar *42*B1
Bulgaria, *c.* 900 *37*D4
   1230 *40*D-E2–3
   1265 *52*B1   1355 *53*B4
   1453 *60*C2   1556 *57*E3
   1701 *71*F4   1721 *76*F4
   1812 *86*E4   1878 *93*B-C2
   1912–13 *94*C5   1914–18 *98*D4
   1919–35 *101*C2
   1939–41 *103*C3
   1942–45 *104*D5
   1968 *107*D4
Bulgars
   526 *32*D-E4   814 *33*C3
Bull Run *92*F4
Bunzelwitz *82*E3
Burdigala (*mod.* Bordeaux) *27*D4
Burgos *39*B4, *43*B4, *49*A5
Burgundian kingdom, 526 *32*B3
Burgundian migrations *32*
Burgundy, Domains of, 1429 *51*
Burgundy, Duchy of, 1100 *39*C3–4
   1180–1453 *50*   1429 *51*D5
   16th century *62*D3
Burgundy, Kingdom of, 1100 *39*C4
Burgundy, Lower, *c.* 900 *37*B4
Burgundy, Upper, *c.* 900 *37*C4
Burkersdorf *82*E3
Burma
   1914 *97*D4
   1941–42 *105*A2
   1942–45 *106*A5
   1968 *108*D-E2
Burma Road *106*A5
Burundi *108*B4
Bury St Edmunds *43*B1
Byblos
   1400 B.C. *6*C2   860 B.C. *9*E1
Byzantine Empire
   526 *32*D-F4–5   814 *33*B-D3–4
   c. 900 *37*C-E5   1100 *39*E-F5–6
   1256 *52*   1355· *53*
Byzantine territories, 1100 *40*
Byzantium (*mod.* Istanbul)
   *21*F1, *28*E3

C

Cabinda *96*C5
Cabot, John, route of, 1497 *58*B2
Cabot, John and Sebastian, route of
 1498 *58*B3
Cabral, Pedro, route of
 1500 *58*C5 and D-E4
Cadiz *55*B6
Caelius, Rome *30*D3
Caen *43*B2, *51*B3
Caere *23*C2
Caesarea (Mazaca, *mod.* Kayseri)
 Cappadocia *26*C2
Caesarea (*mod.* Cherchel)
 North Africa *25*C5
Caesarea (*mod.* Kaisariyeh)
 Palestine *29*D4, *41*B5
Cagliari *40*B4, *85*A4
Cahors *43*B3, *51*C5
Cairo *33*D4, *60*C5, *86*F6
Cajamarca *56*D3
Calabria *23*E3
Calais, 1180–1453 *50*
 1429 *51*D3
Calauria *14*C3
Calcutta *79*C2, B4, *80*F3
Calicut (*mod.* Kozhikode)
 *58*E4, *79*A2, C2, A5, *80*D5
California
 1750 *75*A3
 1861–65 *92*A2–4
California Trail *59*A-C3
Caliphate of Cordoba
 (dominions of the Almoravides)
 1100 *39*B6, *54*A-B3
 1180 *54*D-E3
Calvinists in Europe, 1560 *63*
Camarina *16*C3
Cambodia
 1914 *97*E5
 1968 *108*E3
Cambrai *61*B5, *69*E1
Cambridge *43*B2, *51*C2
Camerinum (*mod.* Camerino) *23*C2
Cameroon (Kamerun)
 1914 *96*C4
 1968 *108*B3
Campania *23*C3
Campo Formio *85*C1
Campus Martius (Field of Mars)
 *30*B-C1–2
Canaan *9*E3
Canada, 1750 *75*B2, 1783 *78*E1
Canal du Midi *69*D-E5
Canary Is. *58*C3, *75*C3, *96*A3
Candia (Iraklion) *40*E5
Cannae *25*F3
Cannanore *79*A2, C2
Cannes *86*C4
Canossa *38*C4
Cantabria *29*A2
Canterbury *43*B2, *51*C3
Canton *42*E4, *97*E4
Canute, Kingdom of *39*
Cap de la Hogue *76*B-C3
Cape Bojador *58*C3

Cape Breton I. *75*B2
Cape Chelyuskin *75*E1
Cape Colony, *c.* 1900 *95*A-C2
 1914 *96*C-D6
Cape Comorin *80*E5
Cape Finisterre *86*A4
Cape Hatteras *92*E4
Cape Horn *75*B5
Cape of Good Hope *75*D4
Cape Province, 1750 *75*D4
Cape St Vincent *55*A6
Cape Sunium (*mod.* Sounion)
 *14*C3, *15*D6
Cape Town *95*A2
Cape Trafalgar *86*A5
Cape Verde *58*C3
Cape Verde Is. *58*C3, *75*C3
Capitol, Rome *30*C2, *31*A6
Caporetto *98*C3
Cappadocia, 500 B.C. *10*B-C2
 under Alexander the Great *22*B2
 189 B.C. *26*C2–3
 44 B.C. *28*E-F3   A.D. 117 *29*D3
Caprera *90*B4
Caprese *45*D3
Capua *38*D5
Capua, Duchy of *38*D5
Capuchin monastery, Paris *83*A-B1
Caracas *88*E1
Carales (*mod.* Cagliari) *23*A3
Carberry Hill *65*E1
Carcassonne *39*B5
Carchemish *6*C2
Cardiff *39*B2
Cardigan *65*C4
Careggi *57*C3
Caria, 189 B.C. *26*A3
Caribbean Sea *56*D1
Carinthia
 936 *38*D3   1648 *67*D6
 1701 *71*D3   *c.* 1800 *85*C1
Carlat *62*C4
Carlisle *51*B1
Carmania *22*E4
Carnatic *79*A5, *80*E4–5
Carniola
 1556 *57*D3   1648 *67*D6
 1701 *71*D3   *c.* 1800 *85*D1
Carolina, 1700 *77*B2
 See also North Carolina and South
 Carolina
Caroline Is.
 c. 1600 *58*F4   1968 *108*F3
Carpathian Mts. *100*E-F4–5
Carpi (Carpathian Mts.) *29*C2
Carrhae *28*F3
Carrion *55*B4
Cartagena *32*B5
Carthage *25*E4, *28*C4, *29*B3
Carthago Nova
 (*mod.* Cartagena) *25*B4
Carthusian Monastery, Paris *83*B4
Cartier, Jacques, route of
 1534 *58*B-C3   1536 *59*D-E3
Carystus *14*D3, *15*E6

Corregidor *106*B5
Corsica, 264 B.C. *23*A2
  526 *32*C4   *c.* 775 *34*A2
  814 *33*B3   843 *36*C6
  c. 900 *37*C4   1100 *39*C5
  1230 *40*B3   1454 *45*B4
  1556 *57*C4   1701 *71*D4
  c. 1800 *85*A-B3 1815 *87*B4
  1860 *90*B4   1914–18 *98*C4
  1919–35 *101*B2
  1968 *107*B4
Cortez, march of
  1519 *58*A3, *59*C-B4–5
Cortona *35*D2
Corunna (La Coruña) *57*A3
Corvey *38*B1, *43*C2
Cos *26*A3
Cosenza *32*D5
Costa Rica *56*C2
Cotentin *104*B5
Cotrone *38*E6
Coutances *49*B3
Coutras *62*B4
Coventry *49*B1, *103*B2
Craigmillar *65*E1
Crato *55*A5
Crécy *51*D3
Cree Indians *59*C2
Creek Indians *59*C-D4
Crema *45*B2
Cremona *23*B1, *89*B2
Crete *11*E3, *12*
  44 B.C. *28*D4   526 *32*E5
  814 *33*C4   1100 *39*F6
  1230 *40*E5   1265 *52*B3
  1355 *53*B6   1556 *57*E5
  1680 *60*B4   1721 *76*F6
  1812 *86*E6   1914–18 *98*D5
  1919–35 *101*C3 1968 *107*D5
Crete, Sea of *14*C-D4
Crimea *11*E1
  526 *32*E3   814 *33*C2
  1520 *60*D2   1796 *72*B-C5
  1878 *93*E1
Crimea, Khanate of
  1556 *57*F2   1762–96 *72*C5
Croatia, *c.* 900 *37*C4, *38*E4
  c. 1100 *39*D4 1680 *60*B1
  1721 *76*D4   *c.* 1800 *85*D1
  1859 *90*D3
Croats, 526 *32*D3
Crocodilopolis *2*A2

Cro-Magnon *1*A2
Croton (*mod.* Crotone) *21*B3, *23*E3
Crusades, 1096–1270 *40*
Csanad *49*F4 . .
Ctesiphon *8*C4, *10*C3
Cuba *56*C-D1
  c. 1600 *58*B3   1650–1763 *77*
  1750 *75*B3
Cuicul (*mod.* Djemila) *29*B3
Culloden *76*B1
Cumae (*mod.* Cuma) *21*A1
Cumans *39*F3–4
Cumberland (county) *51*B1
Cumberland (river) *78*D3
Cumberland (town) *59*D4
Cumberland Road *59*C-D3
Cunaxa *24*E6
Curia, Rome *31*B5(4)
Curzola *49*E5
Custozza *89*C2
Cuzco *56*D4, *88*E2
Cyclades *14*D3
Cyme *26*A2
Cyprus, *c.* 1400 B.C. *6*B2
  c. 700 B.C. *7*A5
  at the time of Alexander the
  Great *22*B3
  189 B.C. *26*B-C4
  44 B.C. *28*E4   A.D. 526 *32*F5
  814 *33*D3   *c.* 900 *37*E5
  1140 *41*A3   1230 *40*F4
  1265 *52*D2   1355 *53*D6
  1556 *57*F5   1680 *60*D4
  1812 *86*F5   1878 *93*E3
  1914 *96*D3   1914–18 *98*E5
  1919–35 *101*D2
  1939–41 *103*D3
  1942–45 *104*E6
  1968 *107*D-E5
Cyrenaica at the time of
  Alexander the Great *22*A3
  Roman province, 44 B.C. *28*D5
  A.D. 117 *29*C5
Cyrene (*mod.* Cirene) *22*A3, *28*D5
Cyrus (river) *10*C2
Cythera *14*C4
Cythnos *14*D3
Cyzicus *20*E1
Czechoslovakia, 1919–35 *101*B-C1–2
  1938–39 *102*D-E4
  1968 *107*C3
Czestochowa *74*A5

D

Dachau *104*B5
Dacia (Roman province) *29*C2
Dagö, 1100 *39*E1
  1370 *44*E1   1660 *70*D3
  1725 *72*A3   1914–18 *98*D1
Dahomey *108*A3
Dahshur *2*A2

Dakar *96*A4
Dalarna, 1660 *70*B3
Dalmatia
  A.D. 117 (Roman province) *29*C3
  1721 *76*D-E5   1800 *85*D-E2
  1859 *90*D3   1878 *93*A2
Dalnaspidal *65*C2

Damão *80*D3, *97*C4
Damascus *28*F4 1400 B.C. *6*C2
  600 B.C. *7*B6 860 B.C. *9*F2
  500 B.C. *10*B3 1140 *41*C4
Damascus, Emirate of *41*D4
Damietta *40*F5
Danelaw *37*B2
Danish-Norwegian colonies
  1750 *75*
Danube (river) *32*C-E3, *39*C-F3–4
Danubius (*mod.* Danube, river)
  *28*C-D1–2
Danzig
  1370 *44*D4 1660 *70*C5
  1721 *76*E2 1793 *84*D2
  1812 *86*D2 1935–39 *102*E4
Dardanelles *93*C2
Dar-es-Salaam *96*E5
Darjeeling *80*F2
Datis, naval attack of
  490 B.C. *20*
Dauphiné
  1429 *51*E5 1562–92 *62*E4
Davis, John, route of, 1585 *58*C2
Davis Strait *58*B2
Dawson *59*B1
Dax *49*A5
Dead Sea *9*E4
Dead Sea Scrolls, location *9*E4
Deccan *79*C2
Decelea *15*C0
Deir-el-Bahri *5*
Delaware (river) *78*E2
Delaware (state) 1783 *78*E3
  1861–65 *92*F4, *92*E3
Delaware Indians *59*D3
Delft *61*C3
Delhi *42*C4, *80*E2
Delhi, Sultanate of, 1525 *79*A
Delian Confederacy *21*
Delos *14*D3
Delphi *14*B2, *15*A5
Demarcation lines
  of 1494 and 1529 *58*
Dendera *2*B3
Dendermonde *68*B4
Dendra (Midea) *15*B6
Denmark
  c. 900 *37*C2 *c.* 1100 *39*D2
  1370 *44*C3 1556 *57*C1
  1660 *70*A-C1–4 1700 *73*A1
  1721 *76*C-D1–2
  1756–63 *82*C1 1812 *86*C1–2
  1815 *87*B-C2 1871 *91*B-C1
  1914–18 *98*C2 1919–35 *101*B1
  1939–41 *103*B-C2
  1942–45 *104*B-C4
  1968 *107*B2
Denver *92*B3
Deptford, London *66*E6
Derby *65*D4
Des Moines *92*C3
Desna (river) *84*F3
de Soto, route of *59*C4
Detroit *78*D2
Dettingen *76*D3

Deva (*mod.* Chester) *29*B1
de Vaca, route of *59*C4
Deventer *44*B4, *61*E2
Devon *51*B3, *65*C5
Diaz, Bartolomeu
  route of, 1486 *58*C4–5
Die *49*C5
Dieppe *69*D1
Digne *49*C5
Dijon *51*D4, *62*D3
Dinant *44*B5
Diois *69*E4
Dionysus, Sanctuary of
  Delphi *19*B5
Dionysus, Theatre of
  Acropolis, Athens *17*D-E5
Dioscurias *11*F1, *29*D3
Diu *79*A2, *80*D3, *97*C4, *108*D2
Diyala (river) *8*C2–3
Djakowo *49*F4
Dnieper (river) *74*D-E5–6
Dniester (river) *73*D3
Dobruja, 526 *32*E3
  1912–13 *94*C-D5
Dodecanese Is., 1912 *94*D6
  1919–35 *101*C2
  1968 *107*D5
Dodge City *59*C3
Dodona *20*A2
Dogger Bank
  battle of 24 Jan., 1915 *98*C2
Dol *49*A3
Dôle *69*E3
Domrémy *51*E4
Domus Caligulae, Rome *31*B6
Domus Tiberiana, Rome *31*C6
Don (river) *72*C-D4–5
Dor *9*E3
Dordogne (river) *51*C5
Dordrecht *44*B4, *61*C3
Dorians *14*
Dorpat *44*E1, *70*D3
Dorset *51*B3
Dortmund *44*B5, *67*B3
Dorylaeum *40*E3
Douai *61*B4, *99*A2
Dover *65*E4
Drake, Francis
  voyage round the world, 1577–80
  *58*A3, B5 and D-E4–5
Drammen *70*A3
Drangiana *22*E3
Drava (river) *76*D-E4
Drenthe *61*E2
Drepanum *16*A2
Dresden *82*D3
Dreux *62*C2
Drogheda *65*B3
Dublin *37*B2, *39*B2
Duero (river) *55*A-C5
Duisburg *44*B5
Dulduli (Hit) *8*B3
Dumfries *65*C2
Dunbar *65*D2
Dundee *65*E1
Dunkirk *61*A4, *99*A1

Dunrobin *65*C1
Dupleix, French territory in
India under, 1741–54 *79*C
Dura-Europus *22*C3, *29*E4
Duranius (*mod.* Dordogne, river) *27*E4
Durazzo *40*D3, *52*A1, *94*A-B5
Durban *95*D2
Durham *39*B2, *65*D3
Durili *8*C4
Durius (*mod.* Duero, river) *25*A3

Dürnstein *39*D3
Durocortorum (*mod.* Rheims) *27*E2
Dutch colonies, 1750 *75*
Dutch East Indies
1941–42 *105*A-B3
Dutch Guiana (Surinam)
1914 *88*E-F1
Dvina (river) *44*E-F2, *84*E-F1
Dybbøl *91*C1

E

East, The, *c.* 600 B.C. *7*
East Anglia *36*B4
Eastern Front, 1914–18 *100*
October 1917 *98*D1–3
Spring 1918 *98*D-F1–3
Eastern Roman Empire
see Byzantine Empire
East Frankish Kingdom
c. 900 *37*C3
East Friesland, 1648 *67*B2
1744 *81*B2   1756–63 *82*B2
East Indies
c. 1600 *58*E4   1750 *75*E3–4
1941–42 *105*A-B3
East Prussia
14th and 15th centuries *74*B4
1618 *81*E-F1–2   1756–63 *82*F1
1865 *91*E1   1914–18 *100*E1
1919–35 *101*C1
1935–39 *102*E4
East Rumelia, 1878 *93*C2
East Slavs *37*D3
Ebro (river) *55*B-D4–5
Eburacum (*mod.* York) *29*B1
Ecbatana (*mod.* Hamadan)
*22*D3, *29*E4, *33*E3
Ecuador, 1533 *56*D3
1811, 1821–31, 1914 *88*E2
Edessa *41*E1
Edessa, County of, 1140 *41*D-E1
Edfu *2*B3
Edgehill *65*D4
Edinburgh *39*B1, *65*E1
Edom *9*E5
Eger, Bohemia *82*C4
Eger (river) *82*C4
Eger (Erlau), Hungary *49*F3
Egmont *61*C2
Egypt, ancient *2*
Egypt
Old Kingdom,
southern boundary *2*A-B4
Middle Kingdom,
southern boundary *2*A4
New Kingdom,
southern boundary *2*A-B5
1400 B.C. *6*A-C2–4
700 B.C. *7*A6
500 B.C. *10*A-B4–5

under Alexander the Great *22*A-B4
44 B.C. *28*E-F5
A.D. 117 *29*D5
656–814 *33*D4–5
1453–1680 *60*C5
1812 *86*F6   1914 *96*D3
1914–18 *98*D-E5
1919–35 *101*D2
1942–45 *104*D-E6
1968 *108*B2
Egypt, Lower *2*A1
Egypt, Upper *2*B3
Ehrensdorf *1*A1
Eichstätt *49*D3
Eichstätt, Bishopric of, 1648 *67*C4
Einsiedeln *48*D5
Eire (Republic of Ireland)
1939–41 *103*A2
1942–45 *104*A4
See also Ireland, Irish Free State
Eisenach *39*D3
Ekaterinburg (*mod.* Sverdlovsk) *97*C1
Ekron *9*D4
El Alamein *104*D6
Elam *6*E2–3
Elba, 1454 *45*C3
c. 1800 *85*B2   1859–60 *90*B4
Elbe (river) *81*C-D2–4
Elbing *44*E4, *70*C5
Elea *21*B2
Elephantine I. *2*B3
El Escorial *55*C5
Eleusis *15*C6
El-Fustat (Cairo) *33*D4
Elis (town) *14*A3
Elis (region) *14*A-B3
Elizabeth, Empress of Russia
conquests of, 1741–62 *72*
Ellice Is. *105*D3, *106*E6
El Paso *59*B4
Elverum *103*C1
Ely *43*B1, *51*C2
Embrun *49*C5
Emden *71*C1
Emesa *29*D4
Ems (river) *81*B2–3
Ems (town) *91*B4
Enghien *61*C4
England, 526 *32*B1–2

F

Gabon *108*B3–4
Gades (*mod.* Cadiz) *25*A4
Gaeta *90*C4
Gaetulia *25*C5
Gainsborough *65*E3
Galapagos Is. *56*B3
Galatia, 189 B.C. *26*B-C2
  44 B.C. *28*E3   A.D. 117 *29*D3
Galicia, Spain *55*A4
Galicia, Poland
  1701 *71*E-F2   1756–63 *82*F4
  1772 *84*D4   1812 *86*D-E3
  1914–18 *98*D3, *100*E-F4
Galilee *41*B5
Galilee, Sea of *9*E2–3
Gallia Belgica *27*E-F1
Gallia Celtica *27*D-F2–4
Gallia Cisalpina *25*D-E1
Gallia Cispadana *23*B1
Gallia Narbonensis *27*E-F4
Gallia Transalpina *25*C-D2
Gallia Transpadana *23*A1
Gallipoli *60*C3, *98*D4
Galveston *59*B4
Gama, Vasco da, route of
  1498 *58*C4–5, and D-E4
Gambia, 1750 *75*C3
  1914 *96*A4   1968 *108*A3
Ganges (river) *80*E-F2
Gangra *26*C1
Gap *49*C5
Garda, Lake *45*C1
Garibaldi, expedition against
  the Kingdom of the
  Two Sicilies, 1860 *90*
Garigliano (river) *45*E4
Garonne (river) *51*C6
Garumna (*mod.* Garonne, river)
  *27*D-E4
Gascony, 1100 *39*B4
  1429 *51*B6   1562–92 *62*B4
Gastein *91*C5
Gath *9*D4
Gaugamela *22*C2
Gaul *27*
Gävle *70*C3
Gaza *22*B3
Gedrosia (Baluchistan) *22*E4
Gela *16*B3
Gelas (river) *16*C3
Gelderland, 1579 *61*D-E2
Gelderland, Upper
  1579 *61*D-E3   1715 *81*A3
Gelnhausen *39*C3
Gembloux *61*C4
Genava (*mod.* Geneva) *27*F3
Generality, The, 1648 *68*B-C3–4
Geneva *48*A6
Geneva, Lake of *48*A6
Genghis Khan, Empire of, 1227 *42*
  most important campaigns *42*
Genoa *45*B2
Genoa, Republic of, 1454 *45*A2
  1556 *57*C3–4
  1721 *76*C-D4–5

Genoese settlements in Aegean Sea
  and on Black Sea coast, 1355 *53*
Genseric *32*C5
Genua (*mod.* Genoa) *23*A1
Georgetown *88*E1
Georgia, Asia *60*E3
Georgia, U.S.A., 1763 *77*B4
  1783 *78*D4   1861–65 *92*D4
Gepides, Kingdom of the, 526 *32*D3
Gergovia *27*E3
Gerizim, Mt. *9*E3, *41*B5
German Confederation, 1815 *87*
German Democratic Republic
  1968 *107*B-C3
German East Africa (Tanganyika)
  1914 *96*D-E5
German Empire, 1701 *71*C-E1–3
  1721 *76*   1871 *91*
  See also Germany
Germania, A.D. 117 *29*B-C1–2
Germania Inferior, A.D. 117 *29*B1
Germania Magna *28*C-D1
Germania Superior, A.D. 117 *29*B2
German South-West Africa
  c. 1900 *95*A1   1914 *96*C6
Germany
  526 *32*C-D2–3   843 *36*C-E4–5
  c. 900 *37*C3   936 *38*A-D1–3
  1100 *39*C-D2–4
  1230 *40*D-C1 2
  1370 (North Germany) *44*B-D4–5
  1378–1417 *47*C-E2
  1556 *57*C-D1–3
  during Thirty Year's War
  1618–48 *64*
  1648 *67*
  1701 *71*C-D1–3
  1721 *76*C-D3–4
  during Seven Year's War,
  1756–63 *82*
  1812 *86*C-D2–3
  1815 *87*B-C2–3
  1865–71
  (unification of Germany) *91*
  1914–18 *98*C2–3
  1919–35 *101*B-C1–2
  1936–39 *102*
  1939–41 *103*B-C2
  1942–45 *104*B-C4–5
  1968 *107*B3
Germany, Federal Republic of
  *107*B3
Gettysburg *92*F4
Ghana, 1968 *108*A3
  See also Gold Coast
Ghent *61*B4, *99*B1
Gibraltar (Jebel Tarik)
  *33*A4, *55*B6, *76*B6, *98*B4, *107*A5
Gien *62*C3
Gilbert Is. *105*D3, *106*D6
Gilboa, Mt. *9*E3, *41*B5
Giza *2*A1, *3*
Glandève *49*C5
Glarus *48*D5
Glasgow *43*B1, *65*C2

H

I

J

K

Kiel *44*C4, *91*C1
Kiev *42*A1, *72*B4, *74*D5
Kilkenny *65*B4
Killiecrankie *65*C2
Kimberley *95*B1
Kings, Valley of the *2*A3, *5*
King's road, between
 Susa and Sardes *10*A-D2–4
Kinross *65*E1
Kinsai (*mod.* Hangchow) *42*F3
Kinshasa (Leopoldville)
 *108*B4
Kipr (Cyprus) *37*E5
Kirkholm *70*D4
Kirkuk *8*C2
Kish *8*C4
Kistna (*mod.* Krishna, river) *80*E4
Klara (river) *70*B3
Kobe *97*F2
Koblenz *38*B2
Koburg *63*D5
Kokenhusen *44*F2
Kolberg *44*D4, *82*D1
Kolin *82*D4
Komarov *100*F4
Königsberg *44*E3, *76*E2
Konya *60*D4
Korea, *c.* 1300 *42*F2
 1914 *97*F2
 1941–42 *105*B1
 1942–45 *106*B4
 1968 *108*E1
Kottbus *81*D3
Kotyora *24*C4
Kourland

1370 *44*E3   1660 *70*D4
1721 *76*E2   1795 *84*E1
1796 *72*A3   1812 *86*D1
Kovno *73*C1
Kragerø *70*A3
Krak *41*C3
Krakow *39*E3, *43*D2, *44*E5
Krakow, Republic of,
 1815 *87*C3
Krasnik *100*E3
Krefeld *82*B3
Kremsmünster *36*E5
Kringen *70*A2
Kronborg *70*A4
Kronstadt *72*B3
Kuban (province) *60*D2
Kuban (river) *72*C5
Kufa *33*E3
Kunersdorf *82*D2
Kura (river) *72*D-E6
Kurdistan *24*D5
Kurhesse *91*B-C3
Kuril Is. *97*F1, *105*C1
Kurisches Haff *100*E1
Kurna *2*B3
Kush (Nubia) *2*A-B5
Küstrin *81*D3
Kut *8*C4
Kutno *100*E3
Kuwait, 1914 *96*E3, *97*A3
 1919–35 *101*E2   1968 *107*F6
Kvikne *70*A2
Kwajalein *106*D6
Kweichow *97*E3
Kyffhäuser *39*D3

L

Labrador *58*B2
La Chapelle *1*A2
La Charité, Paris *83*A3
Lachish *9*D4
La Cité, Paris *83*B3
La Conciergerie, Paris *83*B2(5)
Laconia *14*B3
Lade *37*C1
Ladoga, Lake *70*E3
Ladrone (Mariana) Is. *58*F4
Ladysmith *95*C1
Laerdal *70*A2
Lagash *8*C5
Lagos *96*B4
La Grosse *59*C3
Lahore *97*C3
Laibach (*mod.* Ljubljana) *86*D4
Lake of the Woods *59*C3
La Madeleine, Paris *83*A1
La Mancha *55*C5
La Marche *62*C4
Lambaesis (*mod.* Lambèse) *29*B4
Lambeth, London *66*C6
Lamia *14*B2

Lampsacus (*mod.* Lapseki) *11*E2
Lancashire *65*D3
Lancaster (county) *51*B1
Lancaster (town) *51*B1
Landau *67*B4
Landsberg *64*E4
Landshut *82*D5
Langanes *37*A1
Langres *50*E1, *99*C5
Languedoc, 1429 *51*C-D6
 1562–92 *62*C-D4–5
Lanuvium (*mod.* Lanuvio) *25*E2
Laon *43*C2, *51*D3
La Orilla *59*B5
Laos
 1914 *97*E4   1968 *108*E2
La Paz *56*E4, *88*E3
Lapland *70*D1
La Rabida *55*A6
Larach *8*C4
Laredo *59*B4
Larisa *14*B2
La Rochelle *62*B3
Larsa *8*C5

La Salle, route of *59*C3–4
Las Vegas *59*B3
Latin Empire, 1100 *40*
  greatest extent (1204) *52*
Latin States
  1265 *52*   1355 *53*
Latium *23*C2
Latvia, *1919–35 101*C1
  1939–41 *103*C2   1968 *107*C2
Lauenburg, 1865 *91*C2
Laus *16*D1 . .
Lausanne *48*A6
Lausitz, 1630 *64*E5
Lavant *49*E4
La Vérendrye, route of *59*B-C3
Lavinium *21*A1
Lea (river) *66*E6
Lebanon Mts. *9*E1
Lebanon *107*E5
Lechfeld *38*C3
Leeds *65*D3
Leghorn *85*B2
Legnano, Milan *39*C4
Legnano, Verona *85*C1
Le Havre *62*B2
Leicester (town) *65*E4
Leicester (county) *65*D-E4
Leiden *61*C2
Leighlin *49*A1
Leinster *65*B4
Leipzig *43*D2, *64*D5
Leith *65*E1
Lek (river) *68*B3
Le Mans *43*B3, *49*B3
Lemberg (Lvov) *84*E4, *100*F4
Lemnos *20*C2
Leningrad (St Petersburg, Petrograd)
  *101*C1, *104*D4
Leon (town) *43*A4, *55*B4
Leon (kingdom), 1037 *54*D1
  c. 1100 *39*A4, *54*A2
  1180 *54*D2
Leonidaeum, Olympia *18*A2
Leontini (*mod.* Lentini) *16*C3
Leopoldville *see* Kinshasa
Lepanto *57*D5
Leptis magna (*mod.* Lebda)
  *11*C4, *28*C5
Leptis minor (*mod.* Lamta) *11*C3
Le Puy *43*C3, *51*D5
Lerida *39*B5, *43*B4
Lesbos, ancient *14*E2
  1878 *93*C3   1912–13 *94*C6
Lescar *49*B5
Lesna *73*D2
Lesotho (formerly Basutoland) *108*B5
Lesser Armenia, 1140 *40*B-C1
  1265 *52*D2   1355 *53*D5
Le Temple, Paris *83*C2
Leucas *14*A2, *20*A3
Leuctra *14*C2, *15*B5
Leuthen *82*E3
Leven, Loch *65*E1
Lewis and Clark, route of *59*A-C3
Lexington *78*F2
Leyte *106*B5

Lhasa *97*D3
Libau *73*C1
Liberia
  1914 *96*A4   1968 *108*A3
Libreville *96*C5
Libya, 500 B.C. *10*A3
  814 *33*C4
  1914–18 *98*C-D5
  1919–35 *101*B-C2
  1942–45 *104*B-C6
  1968 *108*B2
Libyan Desert *10*A4
Lichfield *43*B1, *49*B1
Liechtenstein, Principality of
  *67*C5
Liège *61*D4
Liège, Bishopric of, 1579 *61*D4
  1648 *67*B3   1756–63 *82*A3
Liegnitz *82*D3
Lierre *61*C3
Liger (*mod.* Loire, river) *27*D-E3
Ligny *86*C3
Liguria *23*A1
Ligurian Republic, 1797–1805
  *85*A-B2
Ligurians *11*B-C1–2
Lille *61*B4
Lilybaeum (*mod.* Marsala)
  *16*A2, *23*C4
Lima *56*D4
Limassol *40*F4
Limburg
  1429 *51*E3   1579 *61*D4
Limerick *65*A4
Limoges *43*B3, *51*C5
Limonum (*mod.* Poitiers) *27*E3
Limousin *69*D4
Lincoln (county) *51*C2
Lincoln (town) *43*B1, *49*B1
Lincoln's Inn, London. *66*B6
Lindau *67*C5
Lindisfarne *37*B2
Lingen (county), 1702–07 *81*B3
Lingen (town) *82*B2
Linz *82*D5
Lipara (*mod.* Lipari) *16*C2
Liparaeae Is. *16*C2
Lippe (river) *68*C3
Lippe, County of
  1648 *67*C3   1871 *91*B3
Lippespring *36*D4
Lisbon *37*A4, *43*A5
Lisieux *49*B3
Lithuania
  1100 *39*E1   1263–1386 *74*
  1370 *44*F3   1556 *57*D-E1
  1660 *70*D-E4–5
  1721 *76*E2   1795 *84*E2
  1796 *72*A-B4
  1919–35 *101*C1
  1939–41 *103*C2
  1968 *107*C2
Little Bighorn *59*B3
Little Falls *59*D3
Little Poland, 1795 *84*D-E3
Little Rock *59*C3

Marshall Is. *105*D2, *106*D5
Marstrand *76*D1
Martinique, 1750 *75*B3
Maryland
    1700 *77*B1   1783 *78*E3
    1861–65 *92*E3, F4
Masovia *74*B5
Massachusetts
    1783 *78*F2   1861–65 *92*E2
Massagetae *22*D-E2
Massawa *96*E4
Massilia (*mod.* Marseille)
    *25*D2, *27*F4
Massinissa, Empire of *25*
Masulipatam (*mod.* Bandar) *79*A2
Masurian Lakes *100*E2
Matrona (*mod.* Marne, river) *27*E-F2
Maubeuge *99*B2
Mauretania, 104–46 B.C. *25*B5
    44 B.C. *28*A4   A.D. 117 *29*A3
    1914 *96*A4   1968 *108*A2
Mauritius *108*C5
Maya civilization *56*C1
Mayan Kingdom
    7th century *56*   1520 *56*
Mayapan *56*B1
Mayfair, London *66*B6
Mazaca (Caesarea, *mod.* Kayseri)
    *26*C2
Mazara *16*A3
Meaux *49*B3, *62*D2
Mecca *33*E5
Mechelen *61*C4
Mecklenburg
    1100 *39*D2   *c.* 1630 *64*D4
    1812 *86*C2   1815 *87*C2
Mecklenburg-Güstrow, Duchy of
    1648 *67*D2
Mecklenburg-Schwerin, Duchy of
    1648 *67*C2   1871 *91*C2
Media *10*D3
Median Kingdom, 600 B.C. *7*
Medici, activities in west and
    central Europe *c.* 1500 *46*
Medina *33*E4
Medinaceli *55*C5
Medina Sidonia *55*B6
Mediolanum (*mod.* Milan) *23*B1
Mediterranean Sea *11*
Meerut *97*C3
Megara, Greece *14*C3, *15*C6
Megara, Sicily *16*C3
Megiddo *9*E3
Meidum *2*A2
Meissen *49*D2, *82*D3
Meissen, March of *38*D2
Mekong (river) *42*E5
Melinde *58*D4
Melita (Malta) *11*C3
Melos *14*D4
Memel (river) *39*E2
Memel (town) *44*E3, *70*D4, *76*E2,
    *102*E3
Memelland, 1939 *102*E3
Memmingen *64*C6, *67*C5
Memnon, Colossi of *5*

Memphis, Egypt *2*A1, *29*D5
Memphis, Tennessee *59*C4, D4
Mende *49*B5
Mentuhotep, Mortuary temple of *5*
Merano *39*D4
Mercia *36*B4
Merenptah, Mortuary temple of *5*
Merida *39*A5
Merseburg *44*C5
Merv *42*B3, *97*B2
Mesopotamia
    at the time of Hammurabi *8*
    under Alexander the Great *22*C3
    Roman province *29*E4
    814 *33*D3
    1680 *60*E4
Mespila (Nineveh) *24*D5
Messana (*mod.* Messina) *16*D2
Messenia *14*B3
Messina *43*D5
    c. 1800 *85*D4   1860 *90*D5
Messina, Strait of *16*D2
Metauro (river) *35*E2
Metaurum *16*D2
Methone *53*A6
Metz *37*C3, *64*B6, *99*C3
Meuse (Maas, river)
    *61*D5, *99*B-C2–4
Mexico
    c. 1600 *58*A3   *c.* 1750 *75*B3
    Mexico, Gulf of *77*
Mexico City *56*A1, *58*A3, *59*B5
Mézières *62*D2
Michigan *92*D2
Michigan, Lake *59*C3, *78*D1–2
Middelburg *68*B4
Middlesex *66*C6
Midea (Dendra) *15*B6
Midway I. *105*D2
Miklagard (*mod.* Istanbul) *37*E4
Milan *43*C3, *45*B1
Milan, Duchy of, 1454 *45*B1–2
    1701 *71*D3–4   1721 *76*D4
Mile End, London *66*D6
Miletus *20*D4
Minden (town) *49*D1, *82*C2
Minden, Bishopric of
    1648 *67*C2, *81*B3
Minerva, Temple of, Rome *31*C5
Minneapolis *92*C2
Minnesota *92*C2
Minoan-Mycenaean territory
    *6*A-B2
Minoans *12*
Minorca
    *55*E5   1701 *71*C5
    1721 *76*C5   1812 *86*B5
    See also Balearic Is.
Minsk *73*D2
Mirandola *45*C2
Mississippi (river) *59*C3–4, *78*D1–3
Mississippi (state) *92*D4
Missouri (river) *59*B-C3, *92*C2–3
Missouri (state) *92*C-D3–4
Misurata *60*A4
Mitanni, *c.* 1400 B.C. *6*C-D2

Pompeii *23*D2
Pondichéry *79*C2, A5, *80*E4
Pontecorvo (state)
   1812 *86*D5   1860 *90*C-D4
Pontecorvo (town) *85*C3
Pont Neuf, Paris *83*B2
Pont Royal, Paris *83*A2
Pontus, 189 B.C. *26*C1
   44 B.C. *28*F3   A.D. 117 *29*D3
Pontus Euxinus (Black Sea) *28*E-F2
Popes, adherents of the, during
   Great Schism, 1378–1417 *47*
Poplar, London *66*E6
Popocatepetl, Mt. *59*B5
Populonia *35*C2
Porta Caelimontana, Rome *30*E3
Porta Capena, Rome *30*D3
Porta Collina, Rome *30*E1
Porta Esquilina, Rome *30*E2
Porta Naevia, Rome *30*D3
Port Arthur *97*E2
Porta Salutaris, Rome *30*D2
Port Elizabeth *95*C2
Porticus Neronis Margaritaria
   Rome *31*C-D6
Portland, England *76*B3
Portland, Oregon *92*A2
Port Royal, France *69*D2
Port Royal, Paris *83*B4
Port Said *96*D3
Port St Simeon *41*C2
Portugal, c. 1100 *39*A5, *54*A2
   1180 *54*D2–3   1476 *55*A5–6
   1556 *57*A4   1701 *71*A4–5
   1721 *76*A5–6   1812 *86*A4–5
   1815 *87*A4
   1914–18 *98*A3–4
   1919–35 *101*A2
   1939–41 *103*A3
   1942–45 *104*A5
   1968 *107*A4–5
Portuguese colonies, 1750 *75*
Portuguese Guinea
   1914 *96*A4
   1968 *108*A3
Portuguese West Africa *see* Angola
Portus Gesoriacus
   (*mod.* Boulogne) *27*E1
Portus Namnetum
   (*mod.* Nantes) *27*D2
Poseidon, Temple of, Delphi *19*B5
Posen (Poznan) *81*D3, *84*D3

Posen (province), 1865 *91*D2
Posidium (*mod.* Al Mina) *11*F3
Posidonia (Paestum) *21*B2
Potidaea *14*C1
Potomac (river) *78*E3
Potosi *56*E5
Potsdam *82*D2
Poznan *84*D3
Praeneste *23*C2
Praesus *12*D
Prague *43*D2, *82*D4
Prasiae *15*D6
Prato *45*C3
Pressburg (Bratislava)
   *39*D3, *43*D3, *71*E3
Prestebakke *86*C1
Preston *65*D3
Pretoria *95*C1
Priene *26*A3
Pripet (river) *84*E-F3
Pripet marshes *72*B4, *100*F3
Pritzwalk *44*C4
Prophthasia *22*E3
Propylaea, Acropolis
   Athens *13*, *17*A4
Provence *39*C4, *62*E5
Providence *59*D3
Prussia, 1100 *39*E2
   1370 *44*E3   1415–1797 *81*
   1660 *70*C-D4–5
   1700 *73*C2   1721 *76*E2
   1756–63 *82*   1812 *86*D2
   1815 *87*B-C2   1865–66 *91*
Prut (river) *39*F3
Prytaneum, Olympia *18*B1
Przemysl *100*F4
Pskov *101*C1
Ptolemy III, Gate of *4*
Pueblo Indians *59*A-B4
Puerto Rico *56*E1, *77*B4
Punic Wars, 264–146 B.C. *25*
Punjab
   1858 *80*D1   1914 *97*C3
Punt *2*B5
Purus (river) *56*E4
Pusan *97*F2
Puteoli (*mod.* Pozzuoli) *23*C2
Pydna *14*B1
Pylus *14*B3
Pyramids, at Giza *3*
Pyramus (river) *41*C1
Pyrenaei Montes (Pyrenees) *27*D-E4

Q

Qatna *6*C2
Quai d'Orsay, Paris *83*A2
Quebec *78*F1, *92*E2
Queen Charlotte Sound *59*A2

Quimper *49*A3
Quirinal *30*D1
Quito
   *56*D3, *88*D2

Romulus, Temple of, Rome *31*C6(12)
Roncaglia, *39*C4
Roncesvalles *33*A3, *36*A6
Røros *70*B2
Rosendal *70*A3
Rosetta *2*A1
Rosheim *69*F2
Roskilde *43*C1, *70*A4
Rossbach *82*C3
Ross River *59*B2
Rostock *43*C1, *44*C4
Rostra, Rome *31*B6(2)
Rothenburg *64*C6, *67*C4
Rotomagus (*mod.* Rouen) *27*E2
Rotterdam *61*C3
Rottweil *67*C5
Rouen *43*B2, *51*C3
Roussillon *69*E5
Rovno *100*F4
Ruanda-Urundi
    see Rwanda and Burundi
Rubico (river) *23*C1
Rüdesheim *39*C3
Rue de Sève, Paris *83*A3
Rue St Denis, Paris *83*B2
Rue St Honoré, Paris *83*A-B1–2
Rue St Jacques, Paris *83*B3

Rue St Martin, Paris *83*B2
Rügen
    1370 *44*C4   1648 *67*D1
    1660 *70*B4   1721 *76*D2
    1756–63 *82*D1   1865 *91*C1
Rügenwalde *44*D3, *81*D2
Ruhr (river) *68*C4
Ruhr Area *102*C4
Rumelia
    1721 *76*F5   1812 *86*E4
Rusaddir (*mod.* Melilla) *25*B5
Russia, 900 *37*D2
    1300–1825 *72*   1721 *76*E-F1–3
    c. 1750 *75*D-F1–2
    1800–1914 (in Asia) *97*
    1812 *86*D-F1–2
    1815 *87*C-D1–2
    1871 *91*E-F1–3
    1914–18 *98*D-F1–3
    See also Soviet Union
Russian Principalities, 1100 *39*
Ruthenia *102*E4
Rütli *48*C5
Rwanda *108*B4
Ryukyu Is.
    1914 *97*F3
    1942–45 *106*B5

S

Saale (river) *44*C5
Saar
    1935 *102*C4   1968 *107*B3
Saarbrücken *91*B4
Sabini *23*C2
Sacramento *59*A3, *92*A3
Sadowa *91*D4
Sagres *55*A6
Saguntum (*mod.* Sagunto) *25*C3
Sahara Desert *96*B3
St Andrews *65*E1
St Asaph *49*A1
St Augustine *78*E4
St Bernard *48*B6
St Bernard, Great *85*A1
St Bernard, Little *25*D1
St Bertrand *49*B5
St Brieuc *49*A3
Saint Cloud *86*B3
St Davids *49*A1
Saint Denis *43*B2, *51*C4
Sainte Chapelle, Paris *83*B2(5)
Saintes *49*B4
St Flour *49*B4
St Gallen *43*C3, *48*D5
Saint Geneviève (Pantheon)
    Paris *83*B4
St Germain *62*C2
Saint Germain des Prés
    Paris *83*B3
St Gildas de Ruis *43*B3
St Gotthard *48*C6

St Helena
    c. 1750 *75*C4
    1945 *108*A4
St Lawrence (river) *59*D3, *78*E-F1
St Lawrence, Gulf of *78*F1
St Louis *59*C3, *78*D3, *92*D3
St Malo *49*A3
St Mihiel *99*C4
St Omer *61*A4
St Paul, Minnesota *92*C2
St Paul's, London *66*C6
St Petersburg (Leningrad)
    *72*B3, *76*E1, *101*C1
St Pol de Léon *49*A3
St Pons *49*B5
St Quentin *61*B5, *62*D2
St Roche, Paris *83*B2(4)
St Thomas *75*B3
St Victor, Paris *83*C4
Saipan *106*C5
Sais *2*A1
Sakhalin, 1914 *97*F1
    1941–45 *105*C1, *106*C4
Sakjegözü *6*C2
Sakkara *2*A1
Salado (river) *56*E5
Salamanca *43*A4, *55*B5
Salamis (island) *15*C6
Salamis (town) *15*C6
Salef (river) *40*F4, *41*A2
Salerno *34*B2, *43*D4
Salerno, Principality of *38*D5

Salisbury *43*B2, *65*D4
Salla *103*C1
Salona (Salonae, Spalato,
   mod. Split) *29*C3, *34*B2
Salonika *76*E5, *93*B2, *94*B6, *98*D4
Salt Lake City *92*B3
Salvador *56*B2
Salzburg (town) *39*D3
Salzburg, Archbishopric of
   1648 *67*D5   1701 *71*D3
   1721 *76*D4
Samara (*mod.* Kuibyshev) *97*B1
Samaria *9*E3
Samarkand *22*E2, *42*C3
Samarobriva (*mod.* Amiens) *27*E1
Samarra *8*B3, *33*D3
Sambre (river) *68*B5
Samnium *23*C-D2
Samoa *105*E3, *106*E6
Samos *20*D4
Samosata *29*D3
Samothrace *14*D1
San (river) *84*E4
Sand Creek *59*B3
San Diego *59*A3
San Francisco *59*A3, *92*A3
Sangarius (*mod.* Sakarya, river)
   *20*F1–2
Sanlucar *55*B6
San Marino *107*C4
San Miguel *56*C3
San Miniato *45*C3
San Remo *102*C5
San Salvador *58*B3
Sans Souci *82*D2
San Stefano *93*D2
Santa Fe *59*B3
Santa Fe Trail *59*B-C3
Santander *57*A3, *102*A5
Santiago, Chile *56*D6, *88*E4
Santiago, Cuba *56*D1
Santiago de Compostela
   Spain *43*A4, *55*A4
Santo Domingo *56*E1
Santos *88*F3
San Yuste *57*A4
Saône (river) *69*E3
Sarai *42*B2
Sarajevo *94*A5
Saratoga *78*E2
Sarawak, 1914 *97*E5
Sardes *20*E3
Sardinia, 264 B.C. *23*A-B2–3
   during Punic Wars *25*D-E3
   44 B.C. *28*C3   A.D. 117 *29*B3
   526 *32*C4–5   *c.* 774 *34*A2–3
   814 *33*B4   *c.* 900 *37*C5
   1100 *39*C5   1230 *40*B3
   1556 *57*C4   1701 *71*D5
   1721 *76*D5–6
   c. 1800 *85*A-B3–4
   1812 *86*C5   1815 *87*B4
   1859–60 *90*   1914–18 *98*
   1919–35 *101*B2   1968 *107*B5
Sardinia, Kingdom of, 1798 *85*
   1812 *86*C5   1815 *87*B3–5

   1859 *89*A1–2   1859–60 *90*
Sarkars *79*A4–5
Sarlat *49*B5
Sarmatia *28*E-F1
Särna, 1660 *70*B3
Saro (river) *26*C3
Saros, Gulf of *15*C6
Saskatchewan, North (river)
   *59*B-C2
Saskatchewan, South (river) *59*B2–3
Sassanid Kingdom, 814 *33*E3
Saturn, Temple of, Rome *31*B6(1)
Saudi Arabia *107*F5, *108*C2
Sava (river) *39*D-E4
Savannah (river) *78*D-E4
Savannah (town) *59*D4, *78*E4
Saverne *69*F2
Savigny *43*B2
Savona *49*C5, *86*C4
Savoy, 1454 *45*A1
   1701 *71*C3–4   1721 *76*C4
   1800 *85*A1   1859–60 *90*A3
Saxon duchies, 1648 *67*C3
Saxons *32*C2
Saxony, Duchy of, 814 *33*B2
   936 *38*B-C1   1100 *39*D2
Saxony, Electorate of, 1630 *64*D5
   1648 *67*D3   1721 *76*D3
   1756–63 *82*C-D3
Saxony, Kingdom of,
   1812 *86*C-D3
   1871 *91*C-D3–4
Scania
   1370 *44*C3   1660 *70*B4
Scapa Flow *98*B1
Schaffhausen *48*C5
Scheldt (river) *61*B4
Schism, the Great, 1378–1417 *47*
Schleswig (town) *64*C4
Schleswig, Duchy of
   1370 *44*C3   1648 *67*C1
   1660 *70*A4   1866 *91*B-C1
Schlüsselburg (Nöteborg) *72*C3
Schmalkalden *57*C2
Schönbrunn *82*D5
Schönhausen *91*C2
Schweidnitz *82*E3
Schweinfurt *67*C4, *104*C5
Schwerin *44*C4
Schwiebus *81*D3
Schwyz (canton) *48*C5
Schwyz (town) *48*C5
Scone *76*B2
Scotland
   c. 900 *37*B2   *c.* 1100 *39*B1
   c. 1650 *65*C-D1–2
   1721 *76*B2
Scots *32*A1
Scutari *93*D2
Scyllacium *16*E2
Scyllaeum *16*D2
Scyros *14*D2
Scythians *22*B1
Seattle *92*A1
Sebenico *49*E5
Seckau *49*E4

Strasbourg *38*B2, *43*C3
Strasbourg, Bishopric of
  1648 *67*B5
Stratford *65*D4
Stresa *102*C5
Stuttgart *67*C4
Stymphalus *15*A6
Styria, Duchy of, 1556 *57*D3
  1648 *67*D E5   1701 *71*D3
  c. 1800 *85*D1   1871 *91*D5
Subiaco *35*E3
Suburana, Rome *30*D3(1)
Sucre *88*E3
Sudan *108*B3
Sudetenland, 1938 *102*D-E4
Sudrøyene (Hebrides), *c.* 900 *37*B1
Suevi, Kingdom of the, 526 *32*A3
Suez *96*D3
Suez Canal *96*D3
Suffolk *51*C2
Sully *69*E2
Sumatra
  c. 1600 *58*E4   *c.* 1750 *75*E4
  1914 *97*D-E5–6   1941–42 *105*A3
  1942–45 *106* A6
  1968 *108*E3
Sumer *8*C5
Sundgau, 1648 *69*F2
Sundsvall *70*C2
Suomussalmi *103*C1
Superior, Lake *59*C3, *78*D1
Surat *79*C2, *80*D3
Surinam *see* Dutch Guiana
Surrey *65*E4
Susa *10*D4, *22*D3
Susiana *22*D3
Sussex *51*C3
Sutton Hoo *32*B2
Svalbard *58*C1
Sveaborg *86*D1
Sverdlovsk *97*C1
Swabia, 936 *38*B3
  1100 *39*C3   *c.* 1630 *64*C6
Swanscombe *1*A1
Swaziland
  1900 *95*D1   1968 *108*B5

Sweden
  1370 *44*D1–2   1560–1660 *70*
  1648 (territories in
  Holy Roman Empire) *67*
  expansion in 17th century *70*
  1700 *73*B-D1
  1721 *76*D-E1–2
  1812 *86*D1–2
  1815 *87*C1
  1914–18 *98*C1
  1919–35 *101*B-C1
  1939–41 *103*C1–2
  1942–45 *104*C4
  1968 *107*C1–2
Switzerland, 1315–1536 (Swiss
  Confederation) *48*
  1701 *71*C-D3   1721 *76*C-D4
  1800 *85*A-B1   1815 *87*B3
  1914–18 *98*C3
  1919–35 *101*B2
  1968 *107*B4
Sybaris *16*E1
Sybrita *12*B
Syene (*mod.* Aswan) *2*B3
Symaithus (river) *16*C3
Syphax, Kingdom of *25*
Syracuse *16*D3, *23*D4
Syria
  860 B.C. *9*F2   600 B.C. *7*B5
  under Alexander the Great *22*B3
  189 B.C. *26*C4
  Roman province 44 B.C. *28*F4
  A.D. 117 *29*D4   814 *33*D4
  1140 *41*   *c.* 1500 *60*D4
  1919–35 *101*D2
  1939–41 *103*D-E3
  1942–45 *104*E6
  1968 *107*E5, *108*B-C2
Syrian Desert *6*C-D3
Syros *14*D3
Syrtis Major (*mod.* Gulf of Sidra)
  *11*D4, *28*C4
Syrtis Minor (*mod.* Gulf of Gabès)
  *11*C4, *28*C4
Systerbäck *70*E3
Szechwan *97*D-E3

T

Tabor, Mt. *9*E3, *41*B5
Tabriz *42*B2, *60*E3
Tagus (river) *25*A3, *55*A-C5
Talavera *86*A4
Tallin *107*C2
Tamerlane, Empire of, 1405 *42*
  most important campaigns of *42*
Tammerfors *101*C1
Tampa *59*C4
Tanagra *14*C2, *15*C5
Tanais *11*F1
Tananarive (Antananarivo) *96*E6
Tanganyika *108*B-C4

Tanganyika, Lake *96*D5
Tangier *33*A4, *55*B6, *98*A4, *102*A6,
  *107*A5
Tanis *2*A1
Tannenberg *74*A4, *100*E2
Tanzania (Tanganyika and Zanzibar)
  *108*B-C4
Taranto *38*E5
Taras (Tarentum, *mod.* Taranto)
  *11*D2, *21*B2, *23*E2
Tarawa *106*D6
Tarentum (Taras, *mod.* Taranto) *23*E2
Tarentum, Gulf of *21*B-C2

U

V

W

Warka *8*C5
Warsaw *73*C2, *74*B5, *103*C2, *104*C5
Warsaw, Grand Duchy of
    1812 *86*D2–3
Warta (river) *82*E2
Wartburg *39*D3
Warwick (county) *51*B-C2
Warwick (town) *51*B2
Washington (state), 1889 *92*A1–2
Washington (town) *92*E3, F4
Waterford *37*B2
Waterloo *86*C3
Wearmouth *43*B1
Weichsel *see* Vistula
Weihaiwei *97*E2
Weimar *64*D5, *102*D4
Weinsberg *39*C3
Weissenburg *91*B4
Wellington, expedition to Spain
    1808–9 *86*
Wells, England *49*A2
Wells, U.S.A. *59*C3
Wenden *70*D4
Wendland *36*D4
Werben *64*D4
Weser (river) *81*B2–4
Wessex, 526 *32*B2
Western Dvina (river) *70*D-E4
Western Front, 1914–18 *99*
Western Powers, 1939 *103*
West Frankish Kingdom
    c. 900 *37*B3–4
West Frisian Is. *68*B-C1
West Indies, *c.* 1600 *58*A-B3
West Irian
    (formerly Dutch New Guinea)
    *108*F3
Westminster, London *66*B6
Westminster Abbey, London *66*B6
Westmorland *65*D3
Westphalia
    c. 1630 *64*C5   1648 *67*B3
    1812 *86*C2   1865 *91*B3
West Prussia
    13th and 14th centuries *74*A4
    1756–63 *82*E1   1772 *81*E2
    1865 *91*E2
    1919–35 *101*C1
West Turkestan, 1914 *97*B-C2

West Virginia *92*D-E3
West Wales *36*A4
Wetzlar *44*B5, *67*C3
Wexford *65*B4
Whitby *32*B1
Whitechapel, London *66*D6
Whitehall, London *66*C6
White Mountain *64*E5
White Russia, 1772 *84*F2
White Sea *72*C2
Wieliczka *74*B5
Wiener-Neustadt *49*E3
Wiesbaden *102*D4
Wight, Isle of *39*B3, *65*D5
Wilderness *92*F4
Wildhaus *48*D5
Wilhelmshöhe *91*B3
Wilhelmsthal *82*C3
Willendorf *1*A2
Wiltshire *51*B3
Winchester *43*B2, *49*B2
Windau *44*E2
Windsor *51*C2
Winnipeg, Lake *59*C3
Winterthur *48*D5
Wisconsin (river) *78*D1–2
Wisconsin (state) *92*C-D2
Wismar *70*A5, *82*C1
Wittenberg *57*C2, *64*D5
Witwatersrand *95*C1
Wolfenbüttel *64*C5
Wollgast *81*D2
Worcester (county) *51*B2
Worcester (town) *39*B2, *65*D4
Worms *38*B2, *43*C2, *67*C4
Wörth *91*B4
Wounded Knee *59*B3
Wroxeter *36*B4
Württemberg *38*B2
Württemberg, Duchy of
    1648 *67*C4–5
Württemberg, Kingdom of
    1812 *86*C3   1815 *87*B-C3
    1871 *91*B-C-4–5
Würzburg *43*C2
Würzburg, Bishopric of
    1648 *67*C4
Wüsterhausen *81*D3
Wyoming *92*B2–3

X

Xerxes' Canal
    *20*C1

Xerxes' expedition against Greece
    480 B.C. *20*

Y

Yalta *104*E5
Yanaon *80*E4, *97*C4

Yangtse-kiang (river) *97*D-E3
Yarmouth *44*A4

Z